Mel Bay Presents

Flatpickin' the Gospels

by Steve Kaufman

Cover picture by Tim Everett

CD CONTENTS

1	When the Roll Is Called Up Yonder [2:12]		13	The Unclouded Day [2:19]
2	The Glory-Land Way [1:45]		14	Sweet Hour of Prayer [3:14]
3	Life's Railway to Heaven [4:02]		15	Precious Memories [4:13]
4	Are You Washed in the Blood? [1:59]		16	Old Time Religion [1:15]
5	Nearer, My God, to Thee [3:27]		17	The Old Rugged Cross [2:34]
6	Faith of Our Fathers [2:27]		18	The Old Gospel Ship [2:30]
7	Near the Cross [3:05]		19	Sweet By and By [2:39]
8	Softly and Tenderly [3:06]		20	Heaven's Jubilee [1:50]
9	The Lily of the Valley [2:20]		21	Just a Closer Walk with Thee [3:03]
10	Where the Soul Never Dies [1:42]		22	In the Garden [3:08]
11	When the Saints Go Marching In [1:19]		23	A Beautiful Life [2:53]
12	What a Friend [4:05]		24	There Is Power in the Blood [1:46]

1 2 3 4 5 6 7 8 9 0

Visit us on the Web at www.melbay.com — E-mail us at email@melbay.com

Table of Contents

Introduction

Welcome to my Flatpicking the Gospels series. The design of this instructional book, along with the tape, is multifaceted. It was written and recorded in order to:

A) make it easy for you to learn these great gospel tunes.

B) teach you the simple melody for these tunes on the guitar.

C) teach you the words to these tunes along with the melodies using the notation or the tablature.

D) teach you how to play the rhythm parts to these songs that include hammer-ons, pull-offs and bass walks. The backup techniques covered in this manual can be used for many different tunes as long as they follow the same chord structure.

E) provide you with an intermediate solo that is comprised of melody embellishments and standard runs that can also be inserted into other songs that use the same chord structure. This is a technique that sounds easier than it really is.

I have recorded the melody just as it is written in the intermediate solo. After that you will hear two improvised variations. The reason for doing the extra improvised solos is to give you a chance to hear how runs and licks are interchangeable. At some point you may hear the runs and licks from one tune found in another tune. Eventually you will see how they fit together in other songs. Practice this technique of patching together solos from runs and licks out of different songs. When you get it down, you will never have to say that you don't know the song.

Be sure to work through my other books. They all tie together and they will make you into a real guitar picker. Have fun with this book and always, if you run into trouble with anything in this book or any of my other publications, write me a note. My Maryville address is listed somewhere in this book or write to me in care of Mel Bay Publications and they will send it on down to me.

Special thanks to Mr. Eugene McCammon for donating his time, effort and research to this project.

Best always,
Steve Kaufman

Understanding the Notation and Tablature System

Tablature: Tablature (for you note readers) is the "paint by number" method of learning a stringed instrument.

Example 1.   <u>The numbers represent the frets.</u> If you see a "1" on a line you are being instructed to hold down the 1st fret. A "0" (zero) represents an open string.

Example 2.   <u>The lines represent the strings.</u> You have 6 horizontal lines written directly under the staff lines. The top line represents the 1st string. The second line represents the 2nd string and the last line, lowest in the tab system represents the 6th string. When you see a number on a line, first understand that the number is telling you which fret to hold down and then count down from top to bottom to the line that the number is written on. This will tell you which string the fretted note is on.

Example 3.   <u>The circled numbers represent the fretting fingers of the left hand.</u> The first set of notes that you see are called <u>Quarter Notes</u> (see example 3). After they are hit they are to last for a <u>whole beat</u> each. They are called quarter notes because it takes 4 of these notes, or 4 quarters, to make a whole measure in 4/4 time.

Example 4.   The next set of notes/tab are called <u>eighth notes</u> (see example 4). They are equal to <u>1/2 of a beat</u> each. It takes 2 eighth notes to equal the length of time that a quarter note would get. <u>8 eighth notes would fill up a whole measure in 4/4 time.</u> 6 eighth notes would fill up a whole measure in 3/4 time. <u>Eighth notes</u> that are beamed together at the top or bottom, are always hit <u>down first</u>—then up. The first eighth note beamed is always down, the next one is up. The first one is down and the last one is up. If you have a full measure of eighth notes, then the first one in the measure is hit down and the last one is hit up. When you finish a measure like this—stop and check to see if you have hit the last note on an up swing.

Example 5.   <u>Is an illustration of other types of timing.</u> The first measure represents 2 <u>half notes</u>. They are called half notes because each one eats up half of a measure in 4/4 time. They last <u>2 beats each</u>. They are written in tablature as a note that is tied to another note. Only hit the first one and wait for another full beat before hitting the next one. In the next measure is a <u>dotted half note</u> and receives 3 beats. It is written in tablature as a number that is tied to two more numbers. You only hit the first note/number and wait the beats out until you can hit anything again. This measure is ending with a 1 beat rest.

   <u>The next measure has a whole note in it.</u> The note lasts for 4 beats and takes up the whole measure; hence the name whole note. In the tab system it is written as a number that is tied to three more numbers. Only hit the first one and wait. As with any note, be sure to keep the pressure down on the fret as long as possible. This will ensure that the note is lasting the proper amount of time and that you won't sound choppy.

Example 6.   <u>Is made up for different types of rests.</u> One beat, two beat and four beat rests.

Hammer-Ons, Slides and Pull-Offs

Example 7.   <u>Represents the hammer-ons (H.O.)</u> These are eighth note hammer-ons. Hit the first note and then propel your left hand's finger onto the fret that is marked. You must attach the hammered note. You don't want to push your finger onto the string—you must shoot it onto the string. The more attack you have, the clearer the hammer-on will be.

Example 8. <u>The slides are written 2 different ways.</u> Both slides written here represent the same function. Fret the 2nd fret and hit the note. Without releasing the fret and tension, slide your finger up to the 4th fret. Whenever you slide, either forward or backward, keep the string pressure down. Don't take your finger off the string or the note will go away.

Example 9. <u>Pull-offs are the opposite of the hammer-ons.</u> Hit the fretted note as you normally would. Then dig your finger under the string and pull it down and off. By digging your left hand's finger under the string you will in essence be plucking the string with the left hand. This will produce the pull-off effect and you will get two notes heard with one note hit.

Hammer-ons, pull-offs and slides do not have to be labeled as such. There is only one way to do a slide, one way to hammer on and one way to pull off. You may come across a place or two where this action was not marked. You must recognize the action and not look for the H.O., P.O. or Sl. markings.

Watch out for your down ups as you perform these techniques. The explanations and diagrams are marked throughout the book. But be careful, if you get your down ups mixed up then a picking crash is inevitable. You may just knock the bark off the tree, but none the less it will cause a break in timing or stumble of some kind.

Playing the Rhythm

The chords are written above or in all of the measures. If you are unsure how to hold, or finger, a chord then follow these steps. Look in the measure with the chord in question. Hold down the group or stack of numbers that are written on the tablature lines. This will be the chord shape that you are to hold. For example; if you are supposed to hold an A7 chord and it is one that you are not familiar with, then look at any measure that has an A7 written above it. Looking at the tablature you will see the first string-open, second string-second fret, third string-open, fourth string-second fret, fifth and sixth strings-open. You can use the tablature to compile the chord that you will need.

I have written in your bass notes and some bass walks. These walks are standard walk-ins that take you from one chord to another. You may choose to skip the walks. If you do, be sure not to skip over the measure. If the song is in 4/4 time then you will need to hit at least 4 things in the measure. In general, I will hit a bass note then a strum and then a bass note and strum. This gives me my four beats. In 3/4 time I would hit a bass then strum, strum giving me all of my 3 beats. Practice your rhythm as much as you practice the lead. Play the chords slowly so that you can get used to changing chords smoothly. Once your right hand starts the pattern of bass, strum bass, strum, then your left hand should keep up with the right and you should not stop for anything. Only play the rhythm as fast as you can change your chords. Take your time, you'll get it.

Understanding The Notation & Tab Examples

1) & 2)

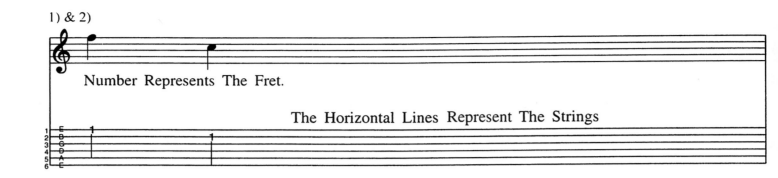

Number Represents The Fret.

The Horizontal Lines Represent The Strings

3) Quarter Notes   4) Eighth Notes

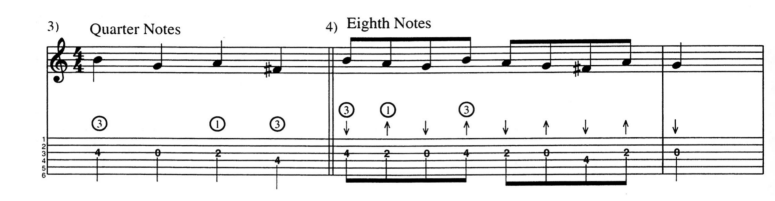

5) Half Notes   Dotted Half Note   Whole Note

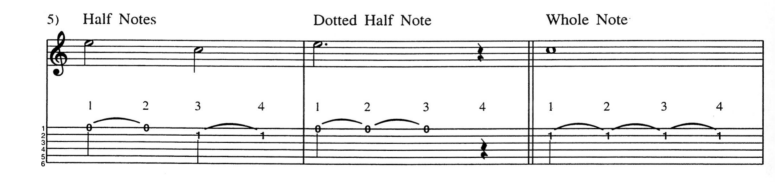

6)   1 Beat Rest   2 Beat Rest   4 Beat Rest

7) Hammer Ons

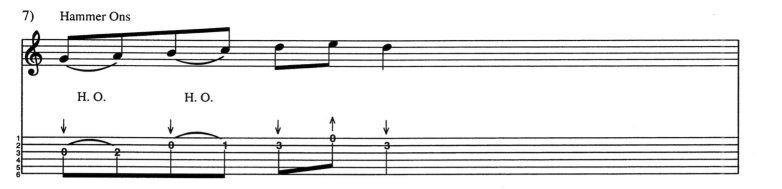

8) Slide   9) Pull Off

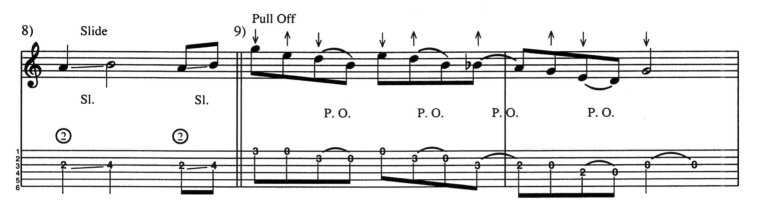

About the Author

Steve Kaufman is the only three-time winner of the prestigious National Flatpicking championships held in Winfield, Kansas. His music covers a broad range of styles including bluegrass favorites, popular swing standards, Irish and Appalachian fiddle tunes, folk and country classics and novelty songs. Steve has been pleasing crowds from California to Austria since 1976, performing a wide variety of acts from educational shows in elementary schools through colleges, to major bluegrass festivals, concerts and television appearances.

Steve keeps busy with his instructional books for Mel Bay Publications, audio and video instructional material for Homespun Tapes, his extensive recording career, his performance and workshop touring agenda and his Maryville private student schedule.

Some of Steve's instructional titles are *Championship Flatpicking*; *The Complete Flatpicking Book*; *Flatpicking The Gospels*; *Bluegrass Guitar Solos That Every Parking Lot Picker Should Know—Volumes 1, 2 and 3*; *Learning To Flatpick;* and *Easy Gospel Guitar*. More titles will be coming out soon.

Steve is pictured on the cover with his Taylor 810 cut-away. Steve plays his 1978 Gallagher 72 Special "Hazel" and his 1992 7-string Gallagher 72 Special cut-away on the *Flatpicking the Gospels* tape that accompanies this book.

When The Roll Is Called Up Yonder

James M. Black

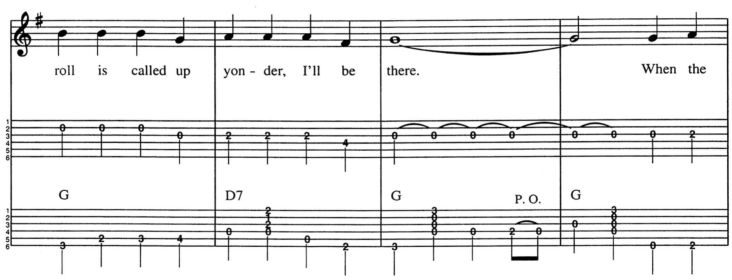

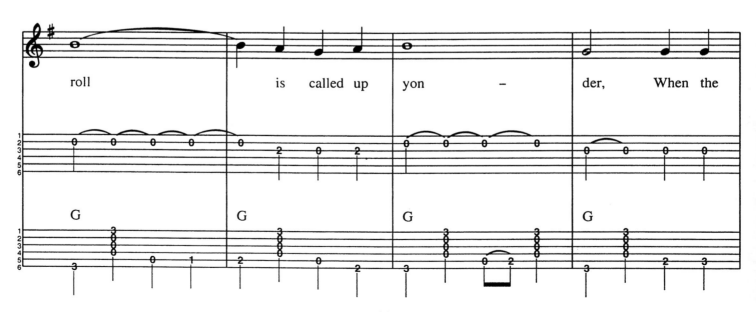

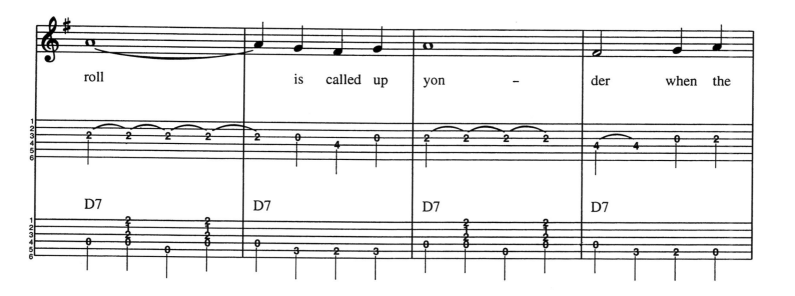

roll   is   called up   yon   –   der   when the

D7   D7   D7   D7

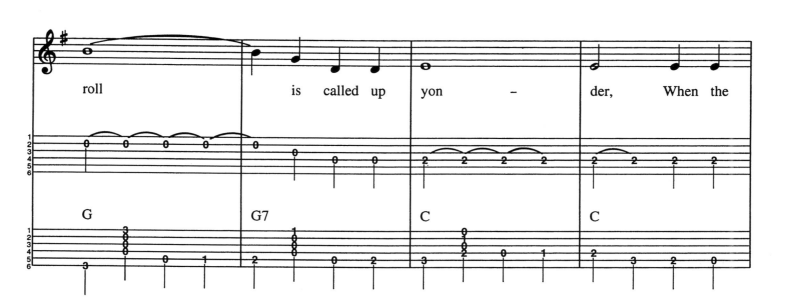

roll   is   called up   yon   –   der,   When the

G   G7   C   C

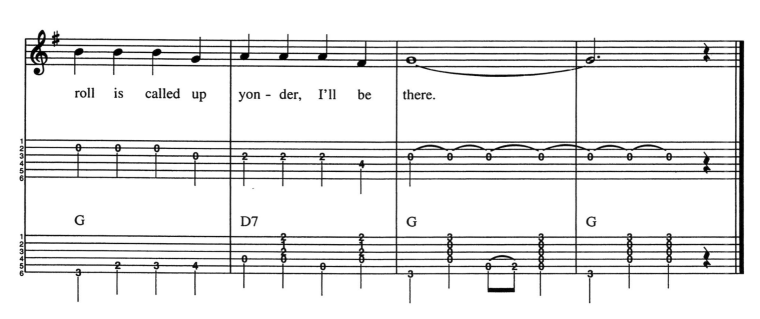

roll is called up   yon - der, I'll be   there.

G   D7   G   G

When The Roll Is Called Up Yonder

Arr. by Steve Kaufman

When The Roll Is Called Up Yonder

1.   When the trumpet of the Lord shall sound,
   and time shall be no more,
   And the morning breaks eternal, bright and fair;
   When the saved of earth shall gather
   over on the other shore,
   And the roll is called up yonder I'll be there.

CHORUS

    When the roll is called up yonder,
    When the roll is called up yonder,
    When the roll is called up yonder,
    When the roll is called up yonder, I'll be there.

2.   On the bright and cloudless morning
   when the dead in Christ shall rise,
   And the glory of His resurrection share,
   When His chosen ones shall gather
   to their home beyond the skies,
   And the roll is called up yonder I'll be there.

    CHORUS

3.   Let us labor for the Master
   from the dawn till setting sun,
   Let us talk of all His wondrous love and care,
   Then when all of life is over
   and our work on earth is done,
   And the roll is called up yonder I'll be there.

The Glory-Land Way

J. S. Torbett

Chorus

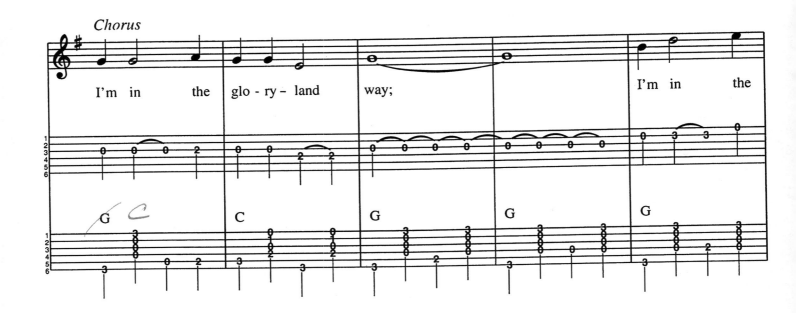

I'm in the glo - ry – land way; I'm in the

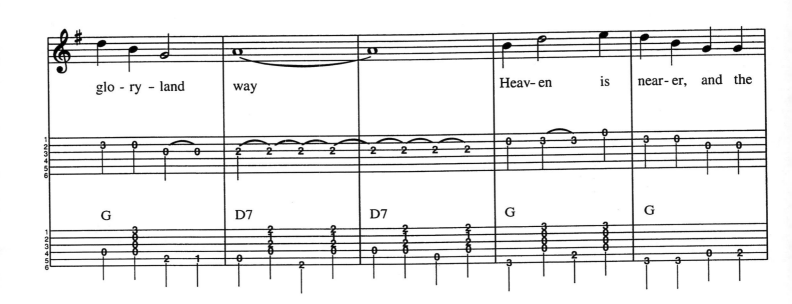

glo - ry – land way Heav- en is near- er, and the

way grow – eth clear- er, For I'm in the Glo-ry – land way.

16

Glory–Land Way

Arr. by Steve Kaufman

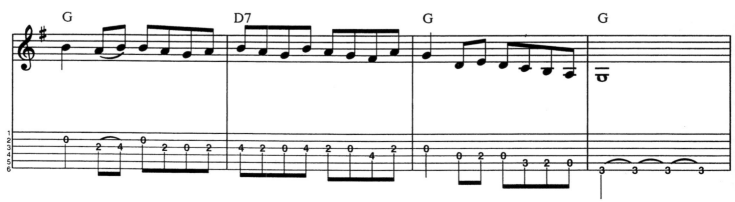

The Glory-Land Way

1.   I'm in the way, the bright and shining way,
I'm in the glory land way;
Telling the world that Jesus saves today, Yes,
I'm in the glory land way.

CHORUS
I'm in the glory land way;
I'm in the glory land way,
Heaven is nearer, and the way grows clearer,
For I'm in the glory land way.

2.   Listen to the call, the gospel call today,
Get in the glory land way;
Wand'rers, come home, oh, hasten to obey,
And get in that glory land way.

CHORUS

3.   Onward I go, rejoicing in His love,
I'm in the glory land way;
Soon I shall see Him in that land above,
Oh, I'm in the glory land way.

CHORUS

Life's Railway To Heaven

Charles D. Tillman

M. E. Abbey

Life is   like   a moun-tain rail-road,   with an

en ___   gi - neer that's   brave;   We must

make   the run suc - cess - Full,   From the

20

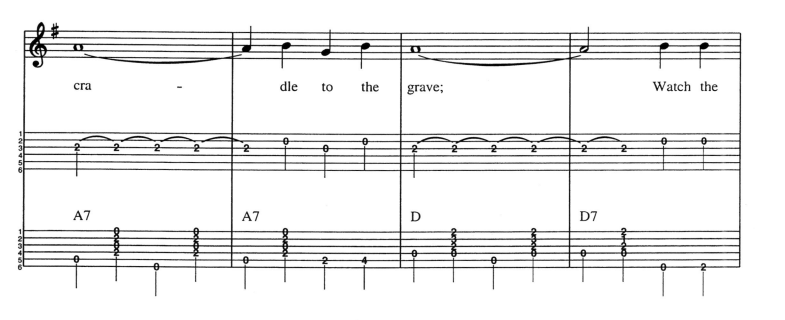

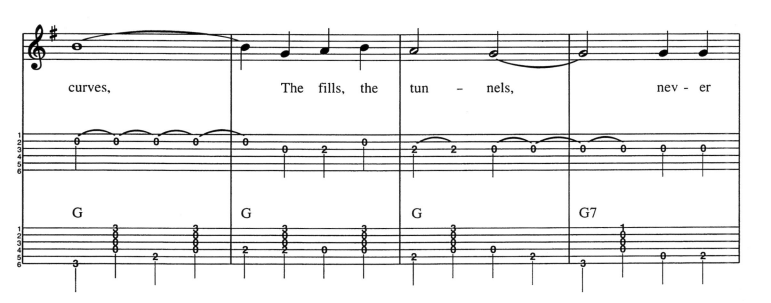

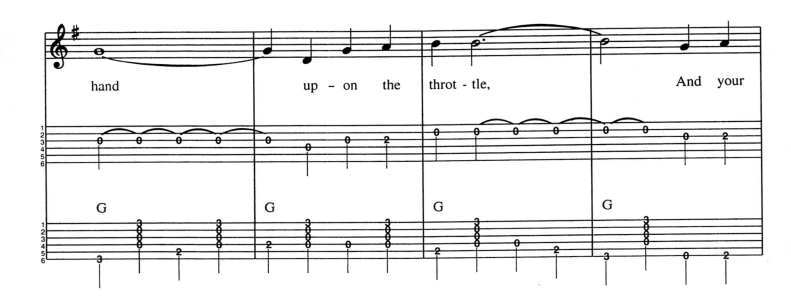

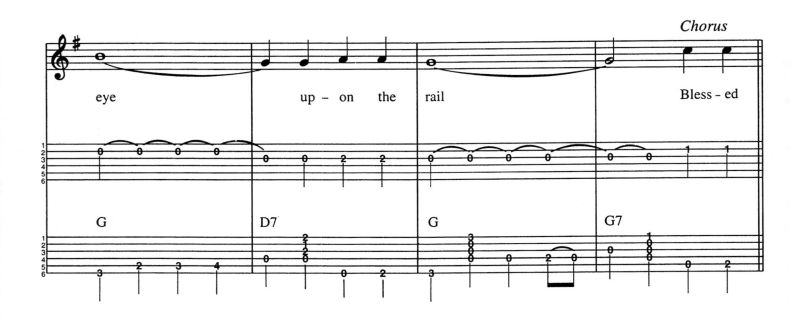

Chorus

22

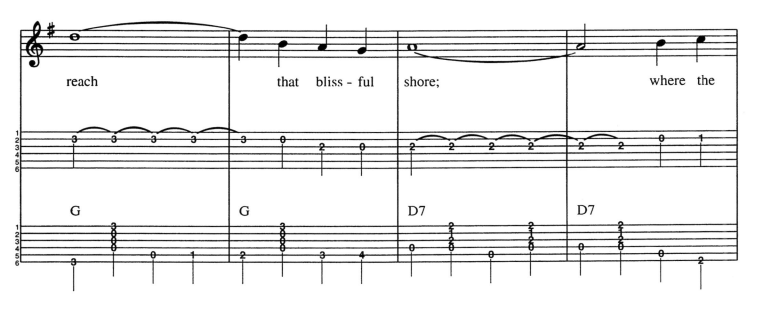

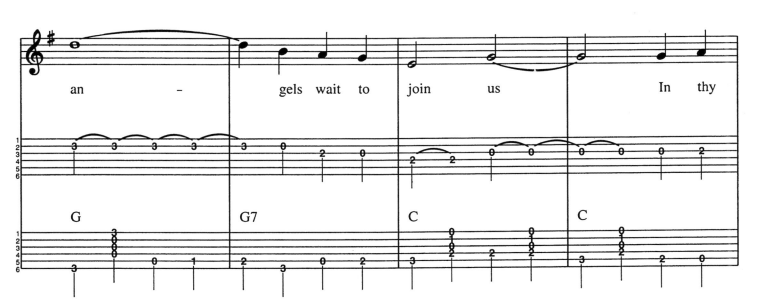

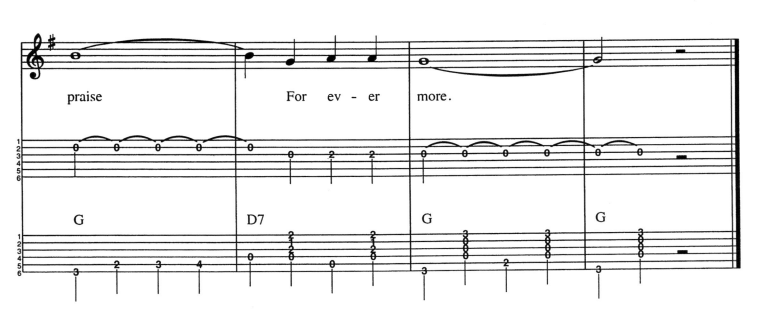

Life's Railway To Heaven

Arr. by   Steve Kaufman

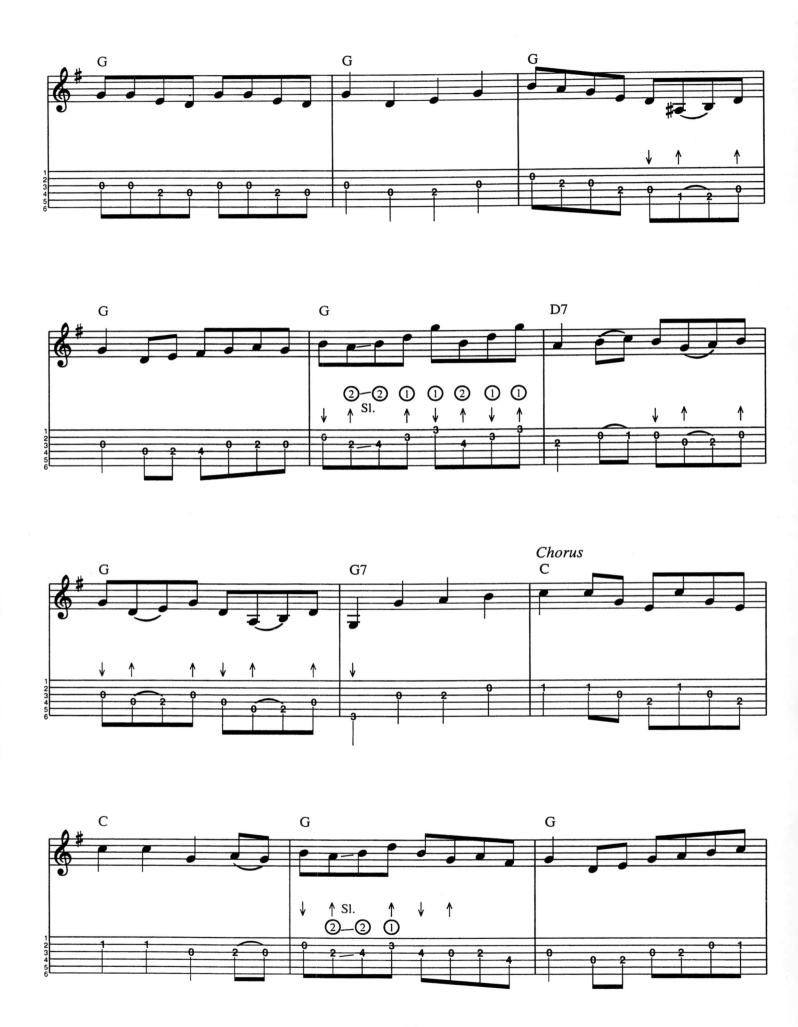

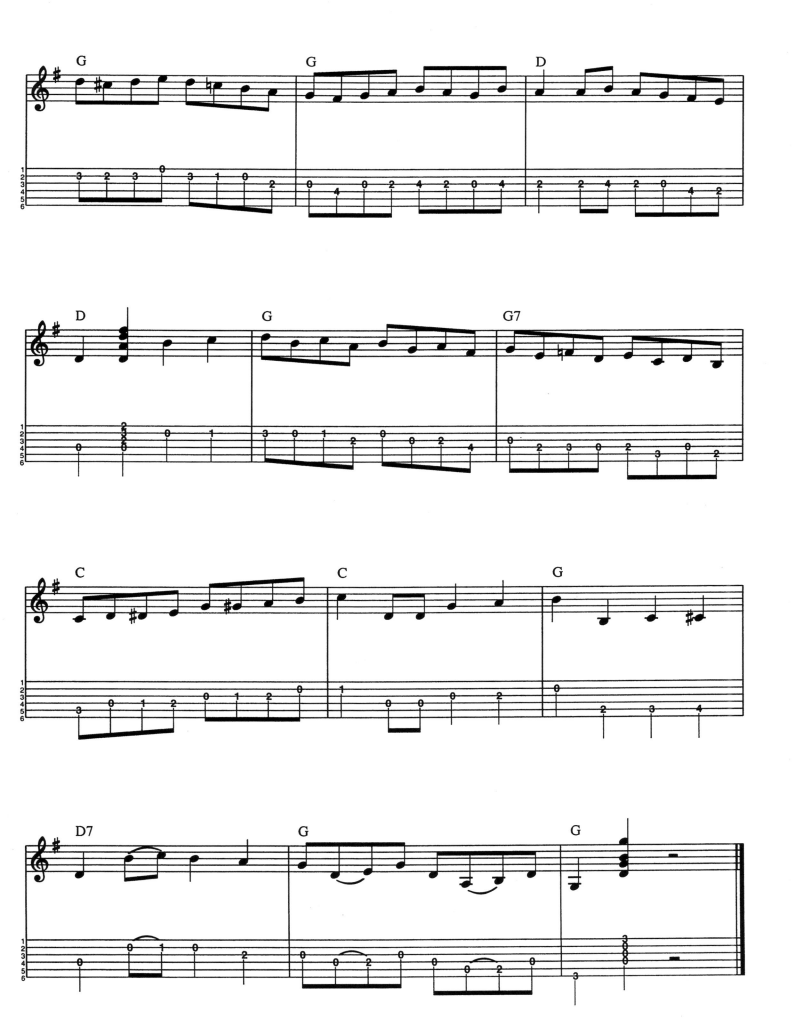

Life's Railway To Heaven

1.   Life is like a mountain railroad,
     With an engineer that's brave;
     We must make the run successful,
     From the cradle to the grave;
     Watch the curves the fills, the tunnels;
     Never falter, never fail;
     Keep your hand upon the throttle,
     And your eyes upon the rail.

CHORUS

     Blessed saviours, Thou wilt guide us,
     Till we reach that blissful shore;
     Where the angels wait to join us
     In Thy praise forever more.

2.   You will roll up grades of trial;
     You will cross the bridge of strife;
     See that Christ is your conductor
     On this light'ning train of life;
     Always mindful of obstruction,
     Do your duty, never fail;
     Keep your hand upon the throttle,
     And your eyes upon the rail.

     CHORUS

3.   You will often find obstructions;
     Look for storms of wind and rain;
     On a fill, or curve, or trestle,
     They will almost ditch your train;
     Put your trust alone in Jesus;
     Never falter, never fail;
     Keep your hand upon the throttle,
     And your eyes upon the rail.

     CHORUS

4.   As you roll across the trestle,
     Spanning Jordan's swelling tide,
     You behold the Union depot
     In to which your train will glide;
     There you'll meet the Superintendent,
     God the Father, God the Son,
     With the hearty, joyful plaudit,
     "Weary pilgrim, welcome home."

     CHORUS

Are You Washed In The Blood?

Capo 2nd Fret
Key Of A

E. A. Hoffman

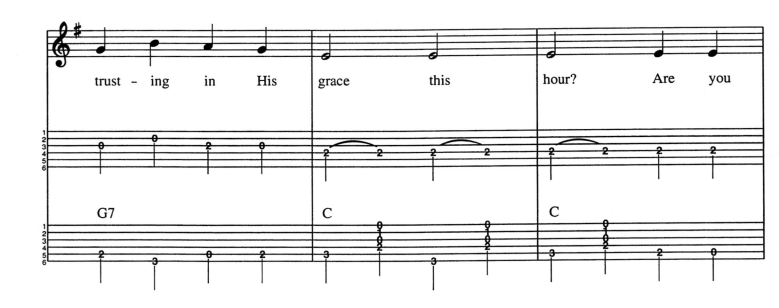

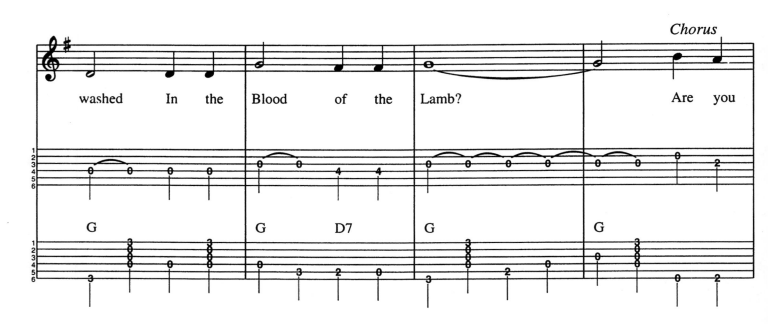

Chorus

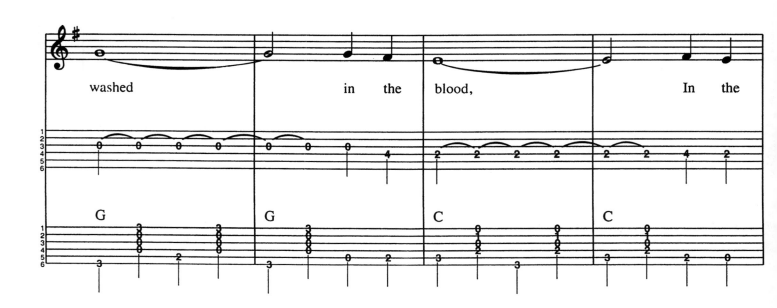

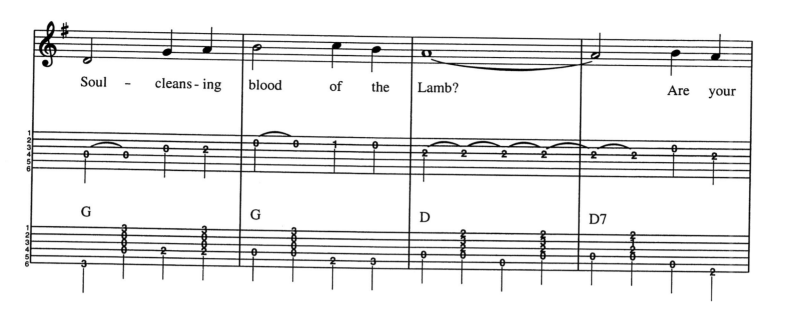

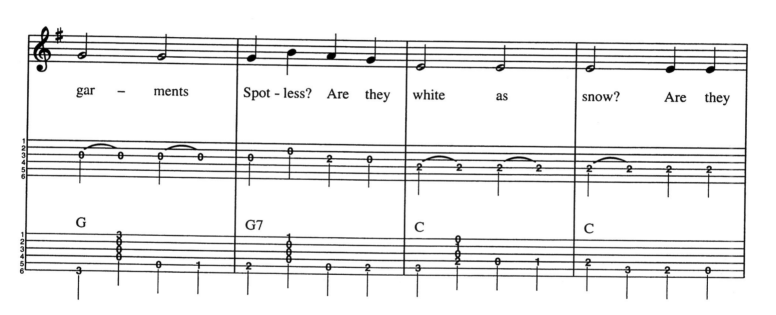

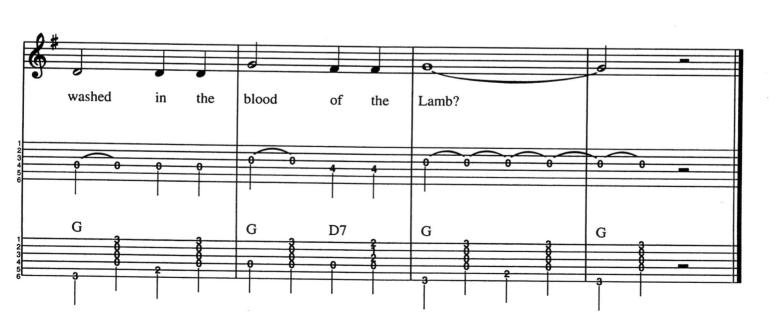

Are You Washed In The Blood?

Arr. by Steve Kaufman

33

Are You Washed In The Blood?

1. Have you been to Jesus for the cleansing pow'r?
    Are you washed in the blood of the lamb?
    Are you fully trusting in his grace this hour?
    Are you washed in the blood of the lamb?

CHORUS

   Are you washed in the blood,
   In the soul cleansing blood of the lamb?
   Are your garments spotless?
   Are they white as snow?
   Are you washed in the blood of the lamb?

2. Are you walking daily by the saviour's side?
    Are you washed in the blood of the lamb?
    Do you rest each moment in the crucified?
    Are you washed in the blood of the lamb?

   CHORUS

3. When the Bridegroom cometh will your robes be white?
    Pure and white in the blood of the lamb?
    Will your soul be ready for the mansions bright?
    And be washed in the blood of the lamb.

   CHORUS

4. Lay aside the garments that are stained with sin,
    And be washed in the blood of the lamb?
    There's a fountain flowing for the souls unclean,
    O be washed in the blood of the lamb!

   CHORUS

Nearer, My God, To Thee

Sarah F. Adams
Lowell Mason

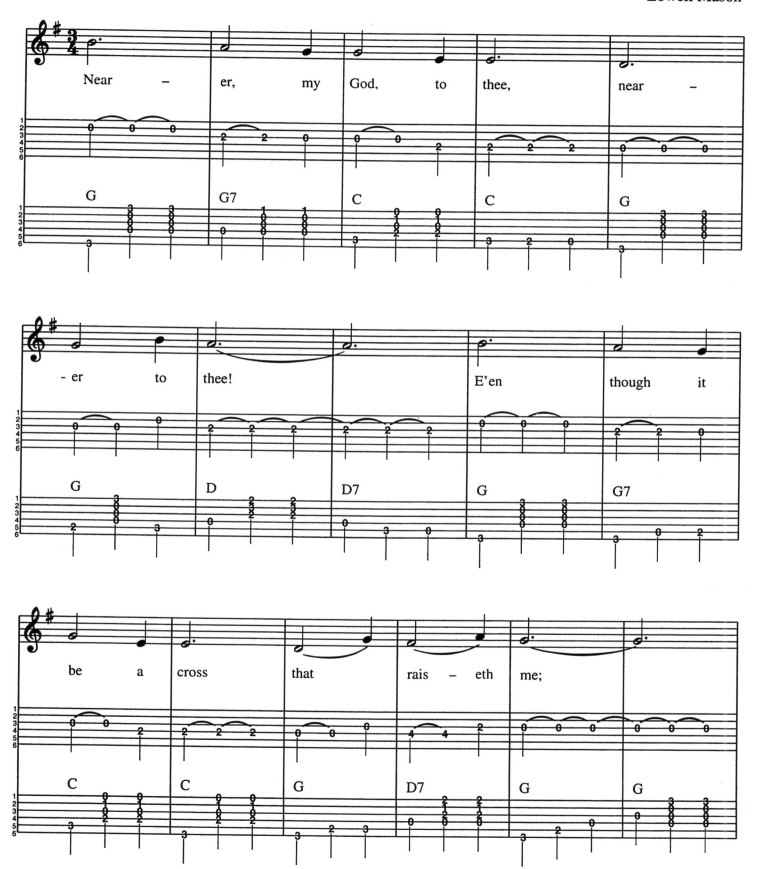

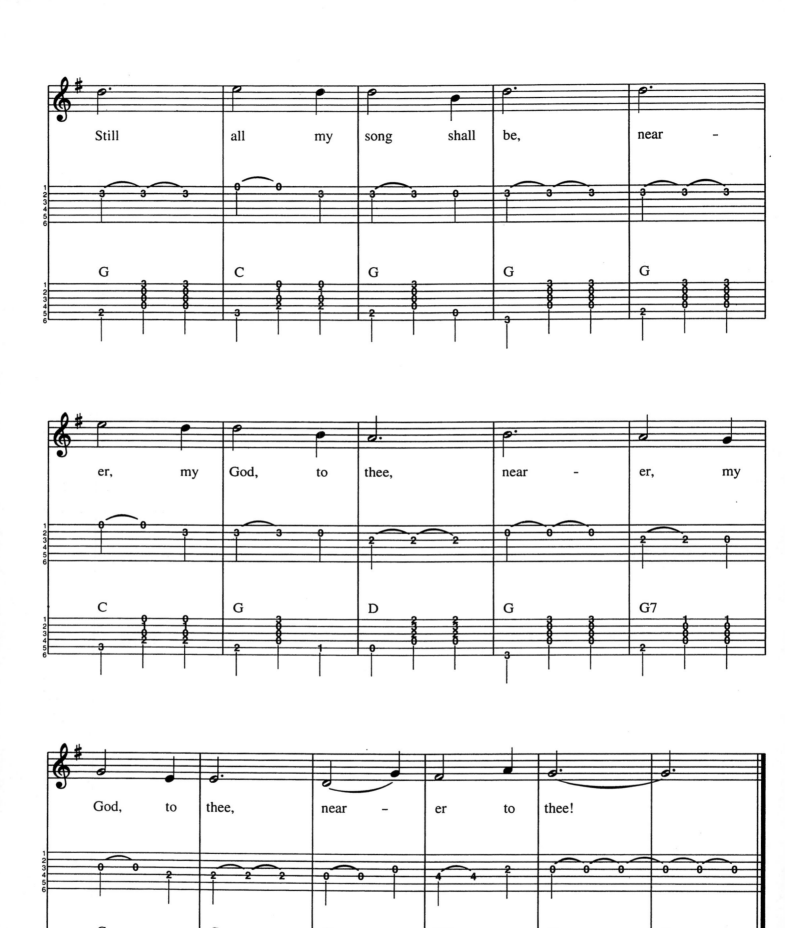

Nearer, My God, To Thee

Arr. by Steve Kaufman

Nearer, My God, To Thee

1.   Nearer, my God, to thee,
Nearer, my God, to thee!
E'en though it be a cross
That raiseth me;
Still all my song shall be,
Nearer, my God, to thee,
Nearer, my God, to thee,
Nearer to thee!

2.   Though like the wanderer,
The sun gone down,
Darkness be over me,
My rest a stone;
Yet in my dreams I'd be
Nearer, my God, to thee,
Nearer, my God, to thee,
Nearer to thee!

3.   There let the way appear,
Steps unto heaven:
All that thou sendest me,
In mercy given:
Angels to beckon me
Nearer, my God, to thee,
Nearer, my God, to thee,
Nearer to thee!

4.   Then with my waking thoughts
Bright with Thy praise,
Out of my stony griefs
Bethel I'll raise;
So by my woes to be
Nearer, my God, to thee,
Nearer, my God, to thee,
Nearer to three!

5.   Or if on joyful wing,
Cleaving the sky,
Sun, moon and stars forgot,
Upward I fly,
Still all my song shall be,
Nearer, my God, to thee,
Nearer, my God, to thee,
Nearer to thee!

Faith Of Our Fathers

H. F. Hemy
Frederick W. Faber

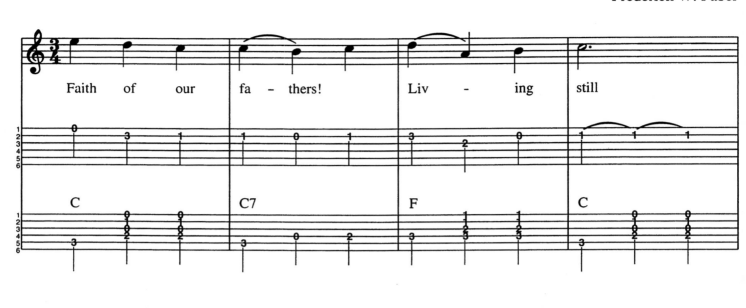

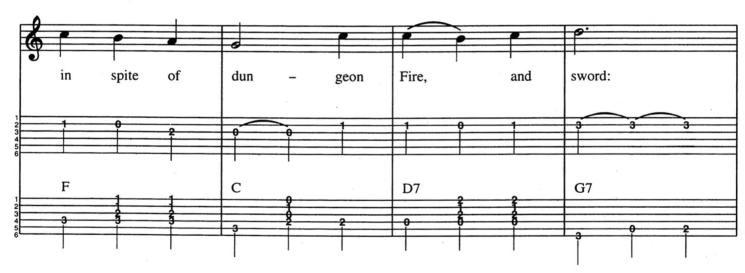

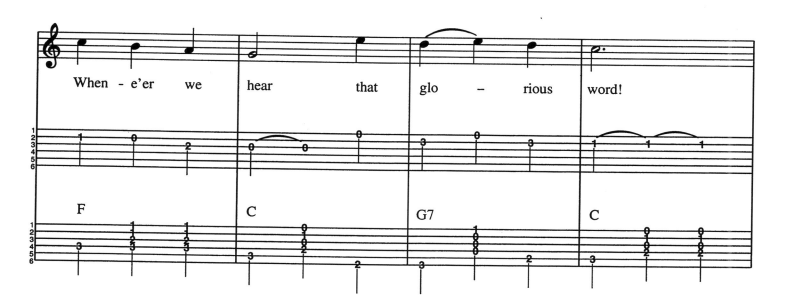

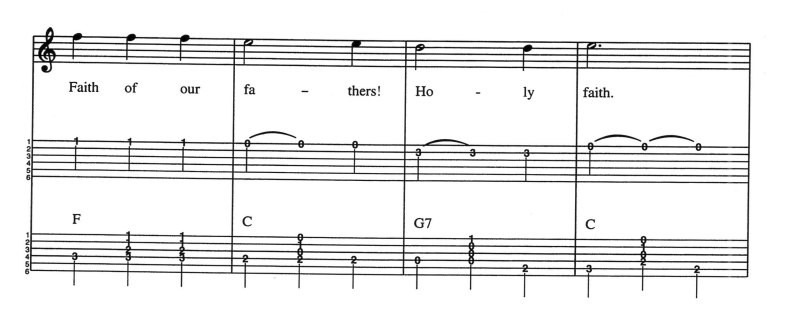

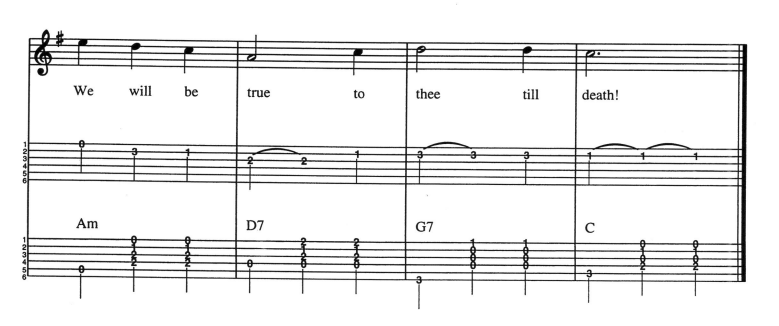

41

Faith Of Our Fathers

Arr. by Steve Kaufman

Faith Of Our Fathers

1. Faith of our fathers! Living Still
    In spite of dungeon, fire and sword;
    O how our hearts beat high with joy
    When e'er we hear that glorious word!
    Faith of our Fathers! Holy Faith!
    We will be true to thee till death!

2. Our fathers, chained in prisons dark,
    were still in heart and conscience free:
    How sweet would their children's fate,
    If they, like them, could die for thee!
    Faith of our Fathers! Holy Faith!
    We will be true to thee till death!

3. Faith of our fathers! We will love both
    friend and foe in all our strife:
    And preach thee, too,
    as love knows how,
    by kindly words and virtuous life:
    Faith of our Fathers! Holy Faith!
    We will be true to three till death!

Near The Cross

Fanny J. Crosby
W. H. Doane

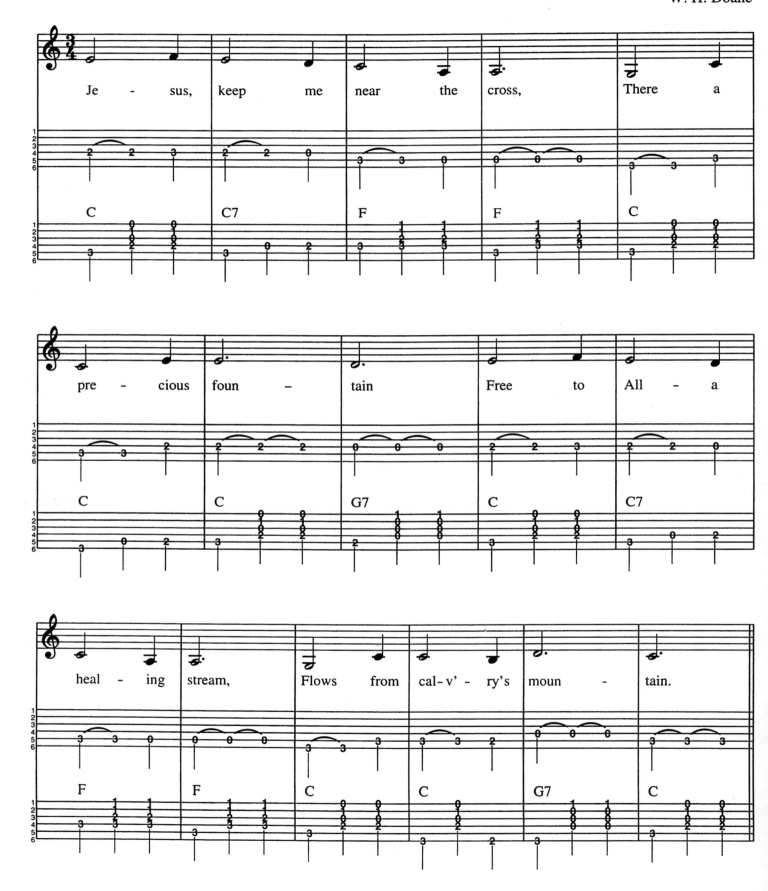

Chorus

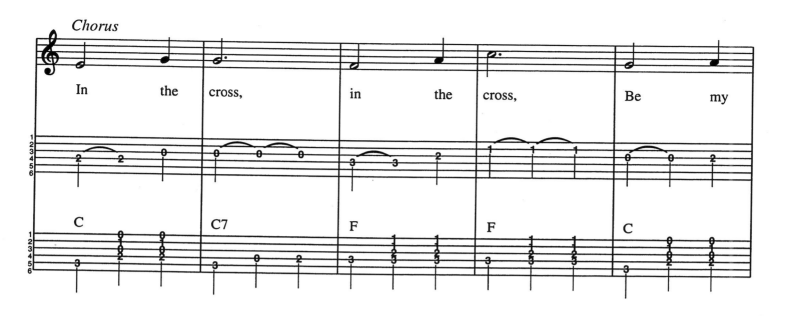

In the cross, in the cross, Be my

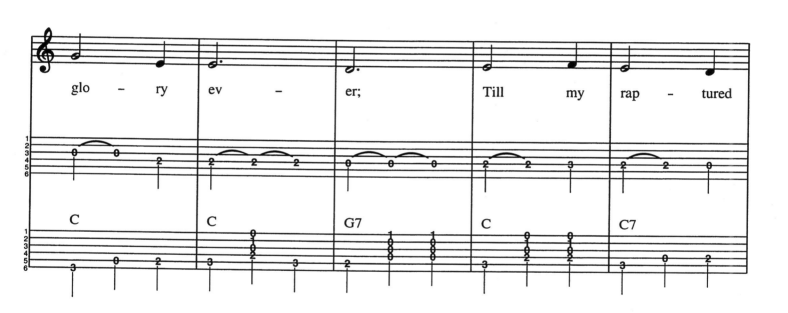

glo – ry ev – er; Till my rap – tured

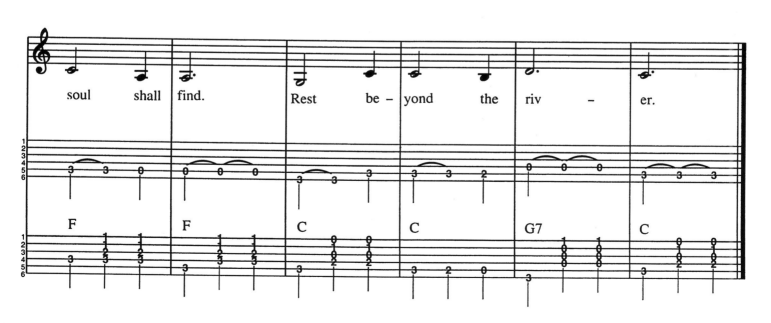

soul shall find. Rest be – yond the riv – er.

Near The Cross

Arr. by Steve Kaufman

Near The Cross

1.   Jesus, keep me near the cross,
      There a precious fountain
      Free to all a healing stream,
      Flows from Calv'ry's mountain.

CHORUS
      In the cross, in the cross
      Be my glory ever;
      Till my ruptured soul shall find
      Rest beyond the river.

2.   Near the cross, a trembling soul,
      Love and mercy found me;
      There a Bright and Morning Star
      Sheds its beams around me.

CHORUS

3.   Near the cross! O lamb of God,
      Bring its scenes before me;
      Help me walk from day to day,
      With its shadows o'er me.

CHORUS

4.   Near the cross I'll watch and wait,
      Hoping, trusting ever,
      Till I reach the golden strand,
      Just beyond the river.

CHORUS

Softly and Tenderly

"Come unto me" – Matt. 11:28

W. L. Thompson

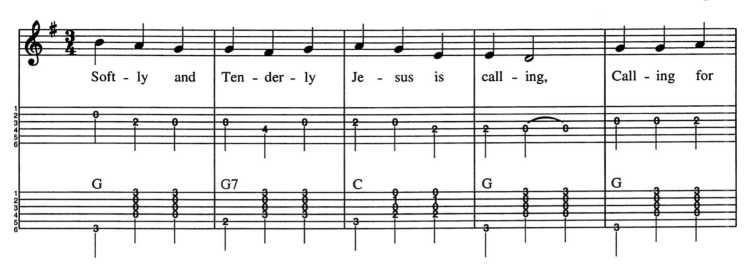

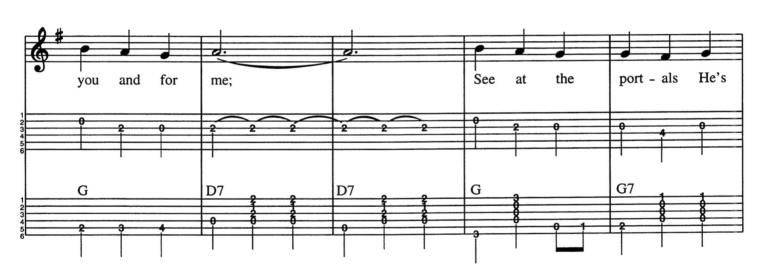

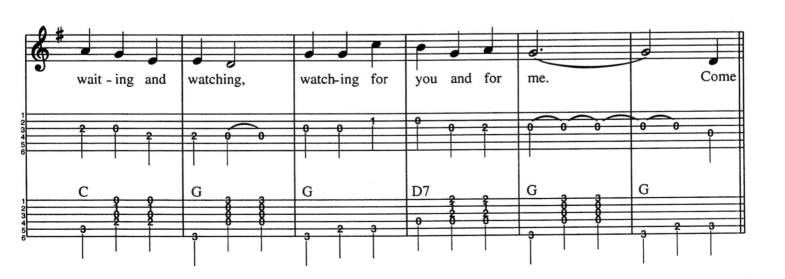

Chorus

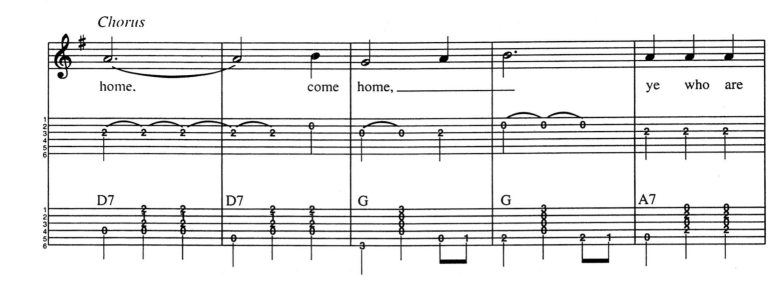

home. come home, _____ ye who are

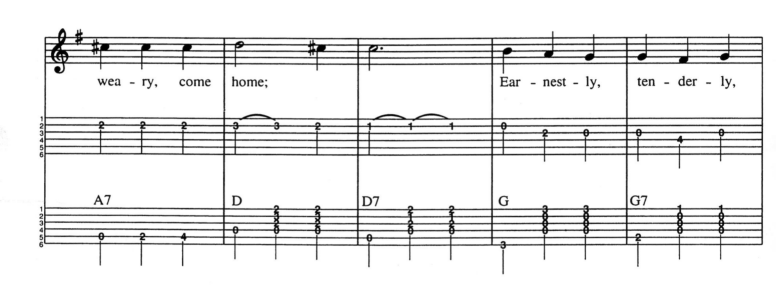

wea - ry, come home; Ear - nest - ly, ten - der - ly,

Je - sus is call - ing, call - ing, O, Sin - ner, come home!

Softly and Tenderly

Arr. by Steve Kaufman

52

Softly and Tenderly

1. Softly and tenderly Jesus is calling,
Calling for you and for me;
See at the portals He's waiting and watching,
Watching for you and for me.

CHORUS
Come home, come home, ...
Ye who are weary, come home;
Earnestly, tenderly, Jesus is calling,
Calling, O, sinner, come home!

2. Why should we tarry when Jesus is pleading,
Pleading for you and for me?
Why should we linger and heed not His mercies,
Mercies for you and for me?

CHORUS

3. Time is now fleeting, the moments are passing,
Passing from you and from me;
Shadows are gathering, death-beds are coming,
Coming for you and for me.

CHORUS

4. O for the wonderful love He has promised,
Promised for you and for me;
Tho' we have sinned, He has mercy and pardon,
Pardon for you and for me.

CHORUS

The Lily Of The Valley

" A friend Loveth at all Times. " Pro. 17:17

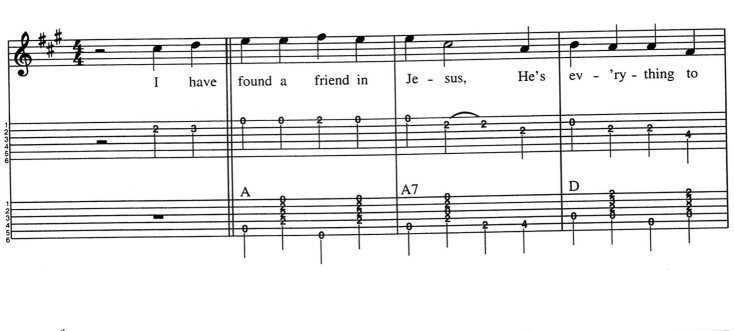

I have found a friend in Je - sus, He's ev - 'ry - thing to

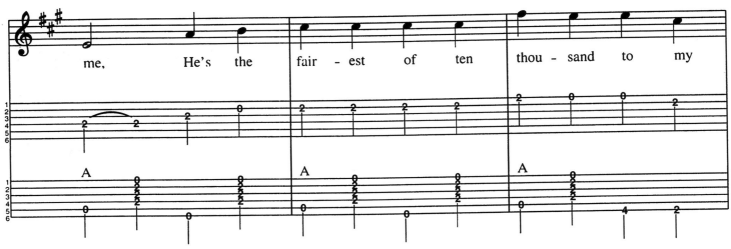

me, He's the fair - est of ten thou - sand to my

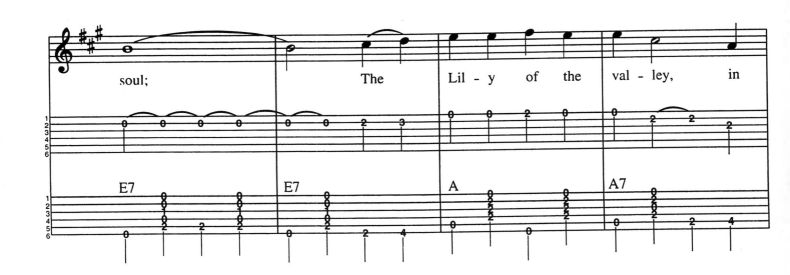

soul; The Lil - y of the val - ley, in

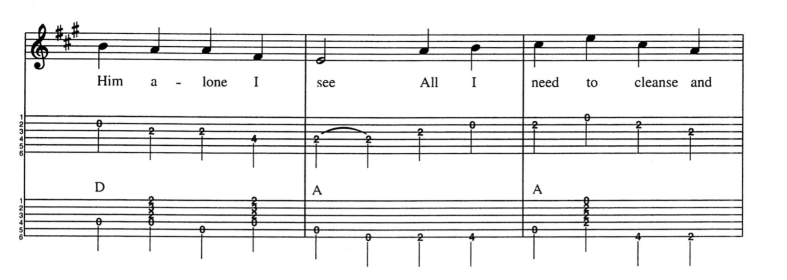

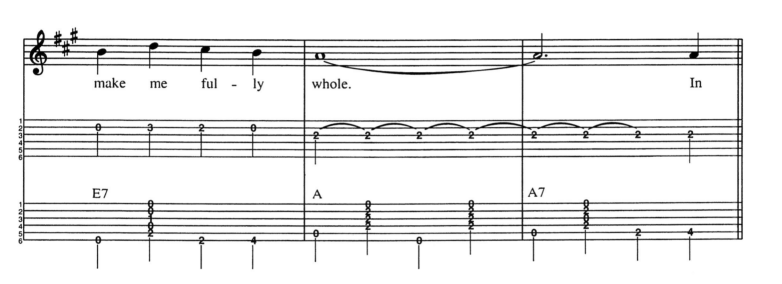

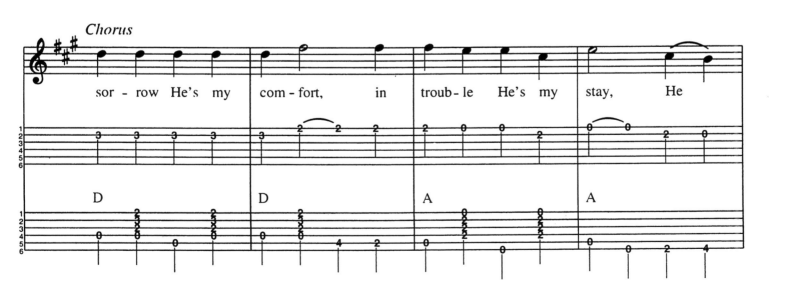

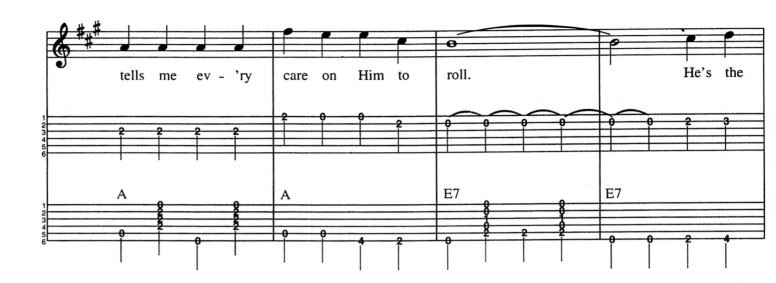

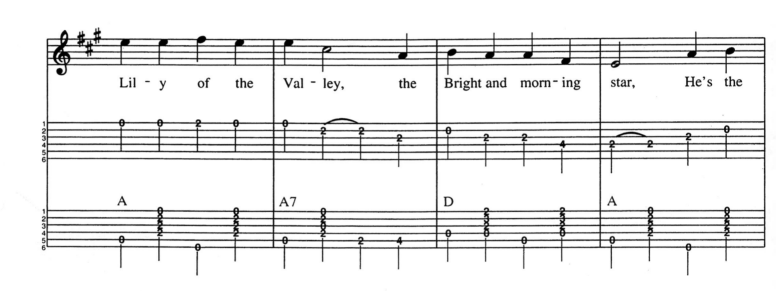

The Lily Of The Valley

Arr. by Steve Kaufman

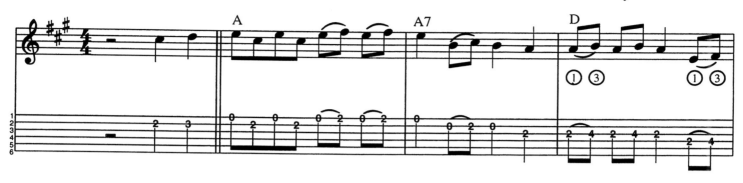

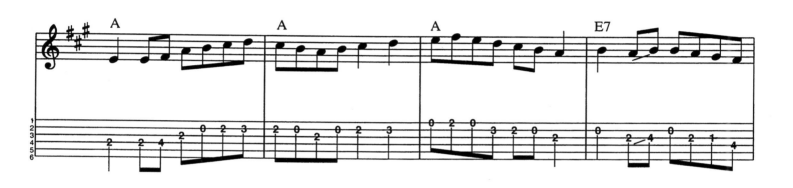

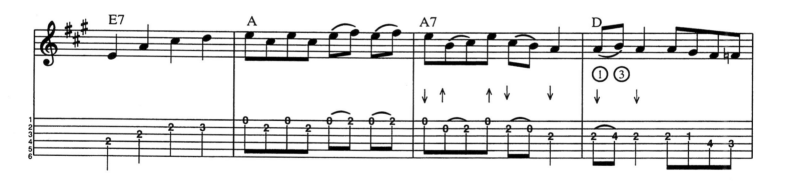

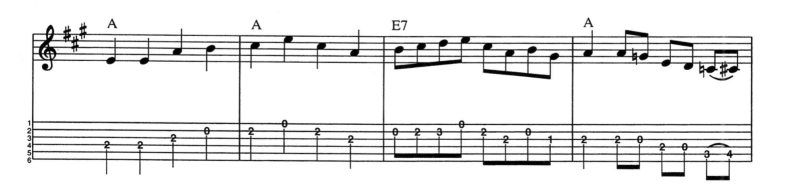

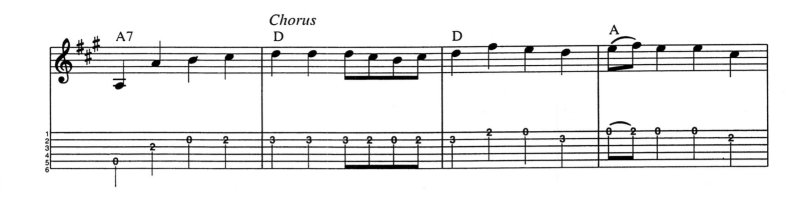

Chorus

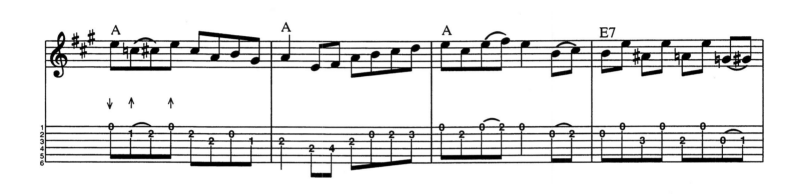

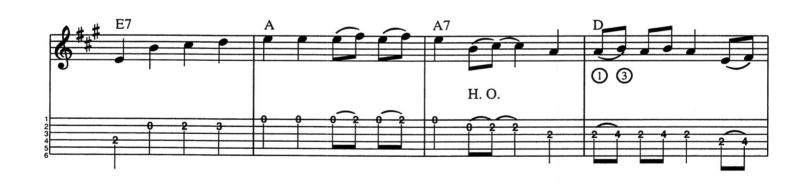

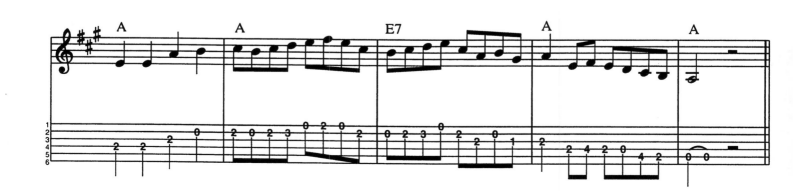

The Lily Of The Valley

1.   I have found a friend in Jesus,
He's ev'rything to me,
He's the fairest of ten
thousand to my soul;
The Lily of the valley,
in Him alone I see All I
need to cleanse and make me fully whole.

In sorrow He's my comfort,
in trouble He's my stay,
He tells me ev'ry care on Him to roll.
He's the Lily of the valley,
the bright and Morning Star,
He's the fairest of ten thousand to my soul.

2.   He all my grief has taken,
and all my sorrows borne;
In temptation He's my strong and mighty tow'r;
I have all for Him forsaken,
and all my idols torn from my heart,
and now he keeps me by His pow'r.

Tho' all the world forsake me,
and Satan tempts me sore,
Thru' Jesus I shall safely reach the goal,
He's the Lily of the valley,
the bright and Morning Star,
He's the fairest of ten thousand to my soul.

3.   He will never, never leave me,
nor yet forsake me here,
While I live by faith and do his blessed will;
A wall of fire about me,
I've nothing now to fear,
with His manner He my hungry soul shall fill.

Then sweeping up to glory,
to see His blessed face,
Where rivers of delight shall ever roll,
He's the Lily of the valley,
the bright and Morning Star,
He's the fairest of ten thousand to my soul.

Where The Soul Never Dies

Wm. M. Golden

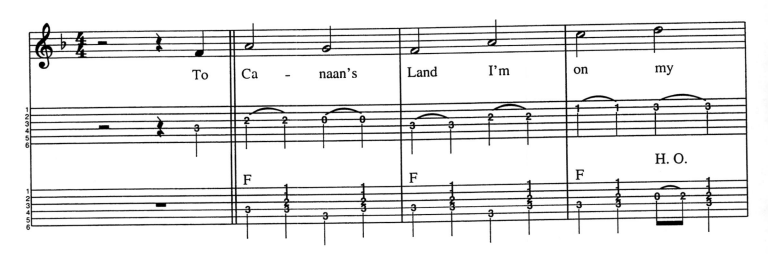

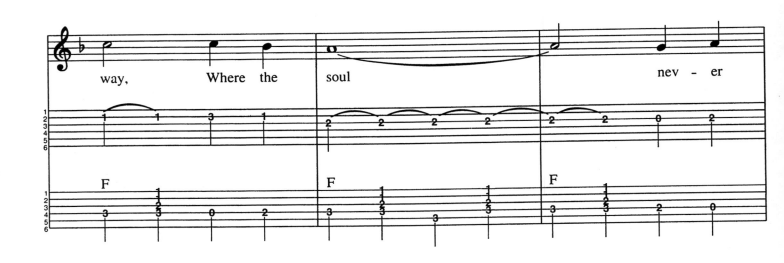

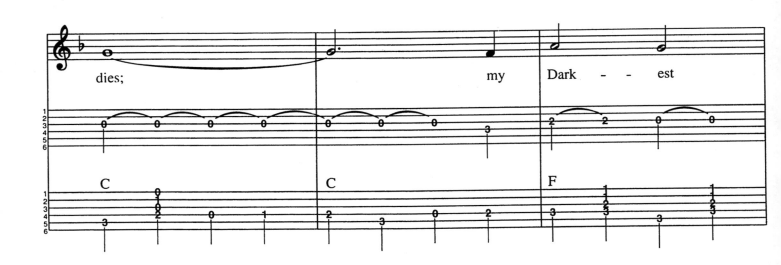

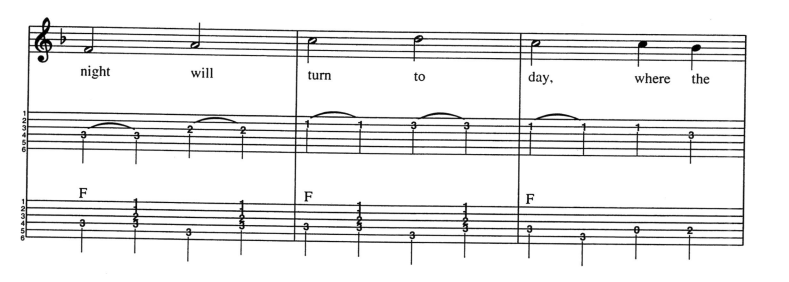

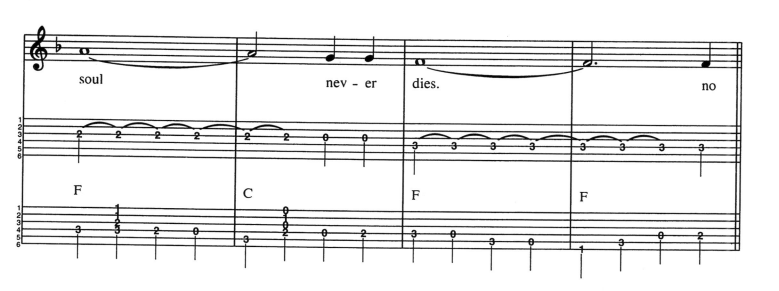

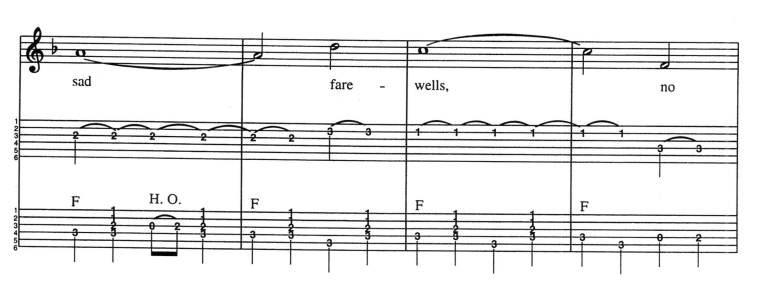

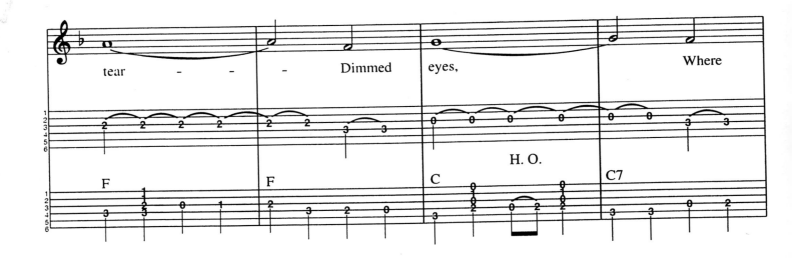

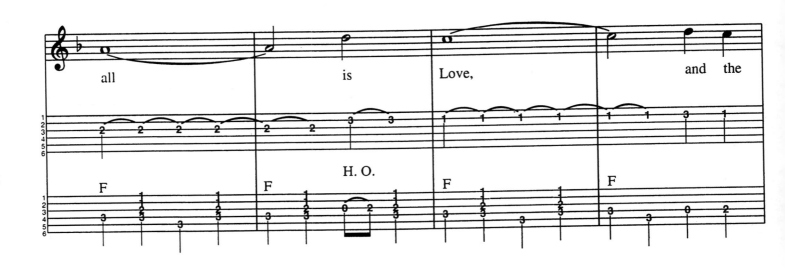

Where The Soul Never Dies

Arr. by Steve Kaufman

Chorus

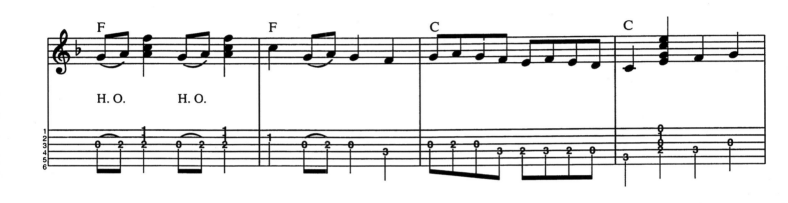

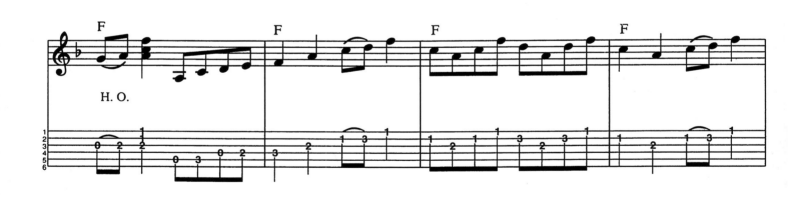

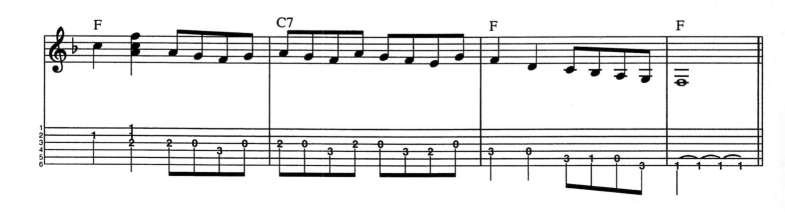

Where The Soul Never Dies

1.   To Canaan's land I'm on my way,
      Where the soul (of Man) never dies;
      My darkest night will turn to day,
      Where the soul (of Man) never dies.

REFRAIN
      No sad farewells,
      no tear dimmed eyes,
      Where all is love,
      Where the soul never dies.

2.   A rose is blooming there for me,
      Where the soul (of Man) never dies;
      And I will spend eternity,
      Where the soul (of Man) never dies.

3.   A love light beams across the foam,
      Where the soul (of Man) never dies;
      It shines to light the shores of home,
      Where the soul (of Man) never dies.

4.   My life will end in deathless sleep,
      Where the soul (of Man) never dies;
      And everlasting joys I'll reap,
      Where the soul (of Man) never dies.

5.   I'm on my way to that fair land,
      Where the soul (of Man) never dies;
      Where there will be no parting hand,
      And the soul (of Man) never dies.

When The Saints Go Marching In

Arr. by Steve Kaufman

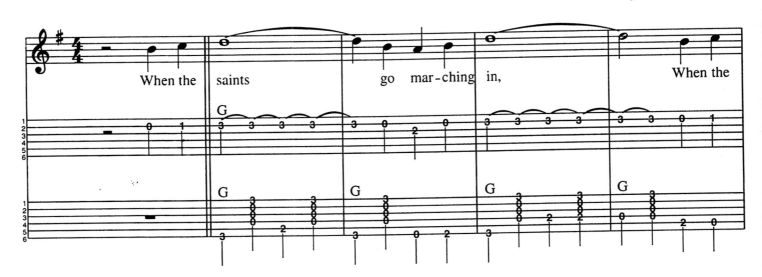

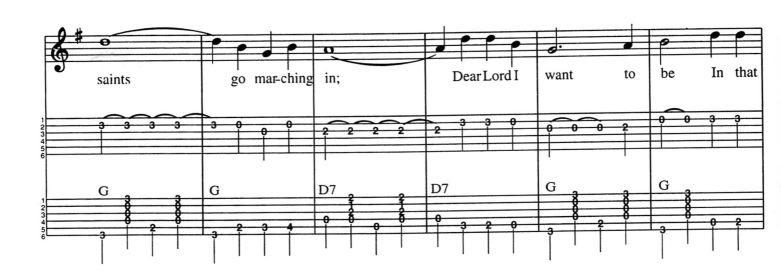

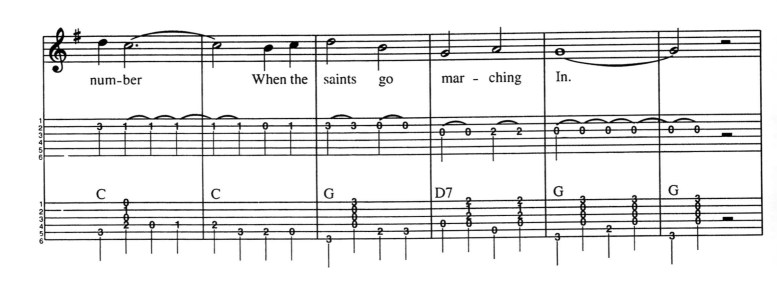

When The Saints Go Marching In

Arr. by Steve Kaufman

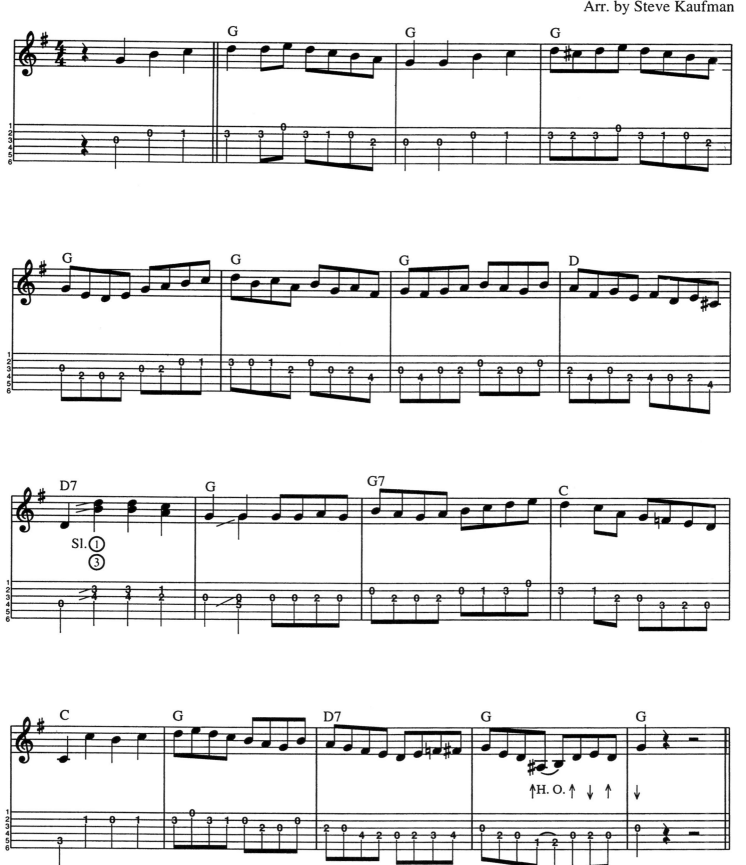

When The Saints Go Marching In

1.   When the sun refuse' to shine,
When the sun refuse' to shine;
Dear Lord I want to be in that number
When the sun refuse' to shine.

REFRAIN
When the saints go marching in,
When the saints go marching in;
Dear Lord I want to be in that number
When the saints go marching in.

2.   When the moon turns into blood,
When the moon turns into blood;
Dear Lord I want to be in that number
When the moon turns into blood.

3.   When we crown Him King of kings;
When we crown Him King of kings;
Dear Lord I want to be in that number
When we crown Him King of kings.

4.   When they gather 'round the throne,
When they gather 'round the throne;
Dear Lord I want to be in that number
When they gather 'round the throne.

5.   While the happy ages roll,
While the happy ages roll;
Dear Lord I want to be in that number
While the happy ages roll.

What A Friend

Charles C. Converse

What a friend we have in Je - - sus, All our

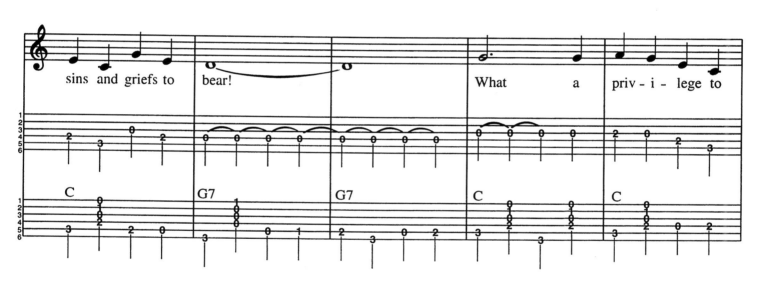

sins and griefs to bear! What a priv - i - lege to

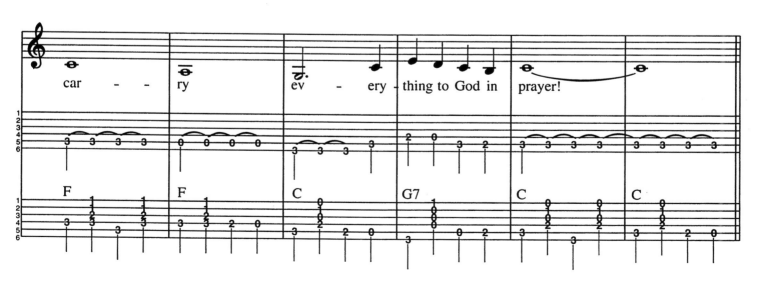

car - - ry ev - ery - thing to God in prayer!

Chorus

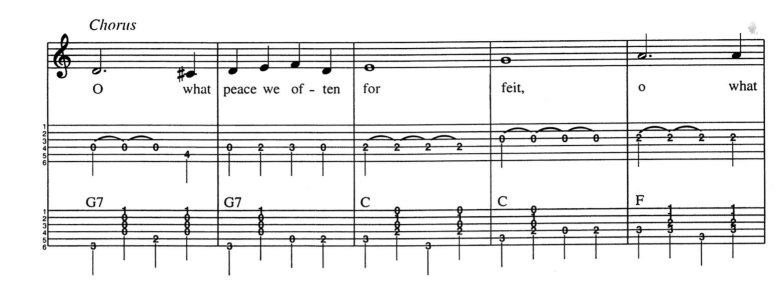

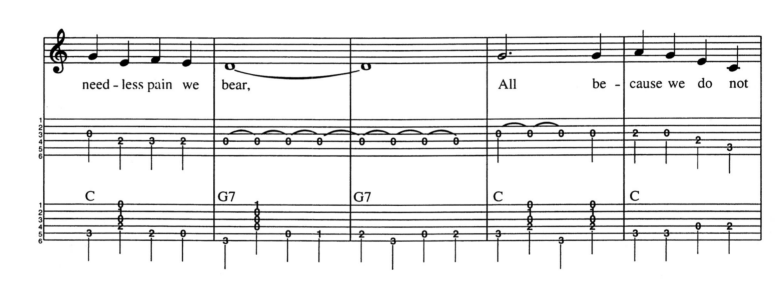

What A Friend

Arr. by Steve Kaufman

What A Friend

1. What a friend we have in Jesus,
   All our sins and griefs to bear!
   What a privilege to carry
   Everything to God in prayer!
   O what peace we often forfeit,
   O what needless pain we bear,
   All because we do not carry
   Everything to God in prayer!

2. Have we trials and temptations?
   Is there trouble anywhere?
   We should never be discouraged,
   Take it to the Lord in prayer.
   Can we find a friend so faithful
   Who will all our sorrows share?
   Jesus knows our every weakness,
   Take it to the Lord in prayer.

3. Are we weak and heavy laden,
   Cumbered with a load of care?
   Precious Savior, still our refuge,
   Take it to the Lord in prayer.
   Do thy friends despise, forsake thee?
   Take it to the Lord in prayer;
   In His arms He'll take and shield thee,
   Thou wilt find a solace there.

The Unclouded Day

Rev. J. K. Alwood

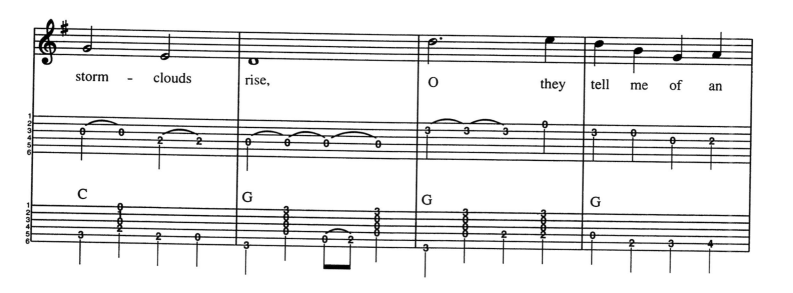

Chorus

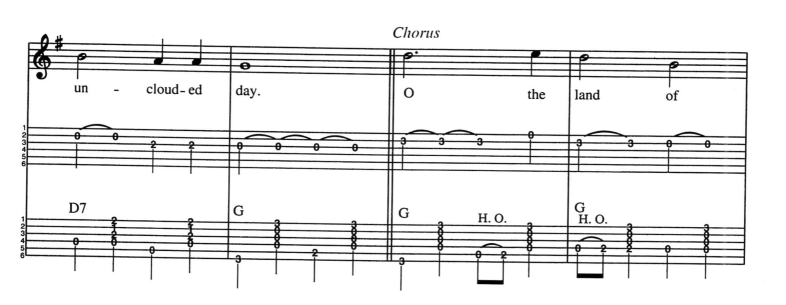

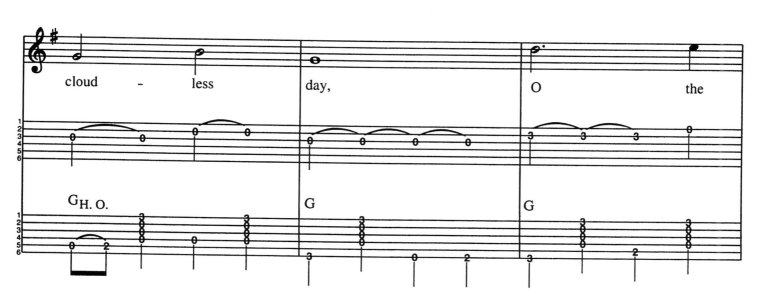

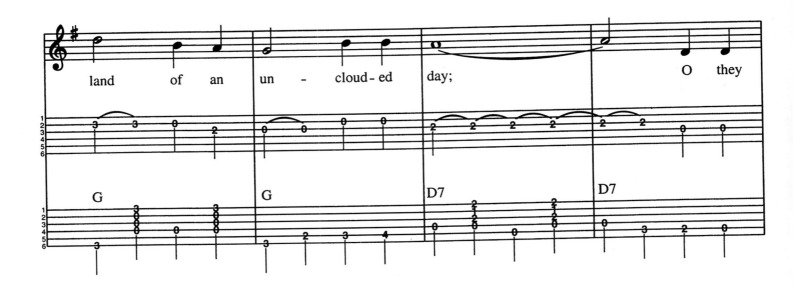

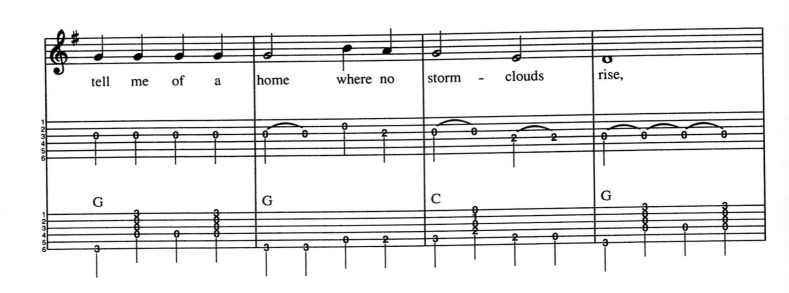

The Unclouded Day

Arr. by Steve Kaufman

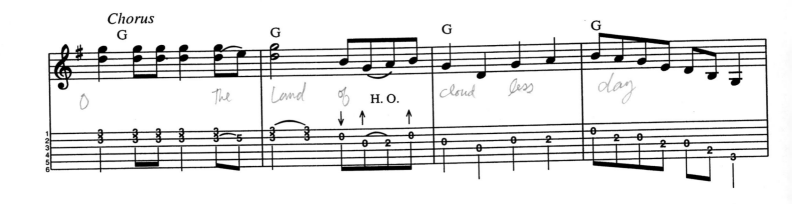

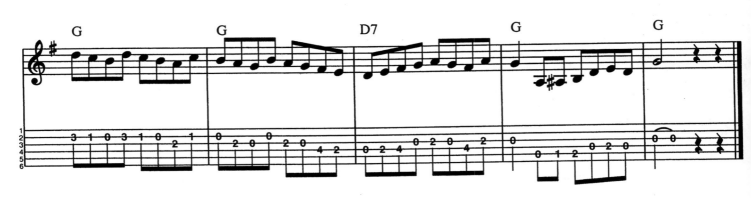

The Unclouded Day

1.   O they tell me of a home
far beyond the skies,
O they tell me of a home far away;
where no storm clouds rise,
O, they tell me of an unclouded day.

CHORUS
    O the land of cloudless day,
O the land of an unclouded day;
O they tell me of a home
where no storm clouds rise,
O, they tell me of an unclouded day.

2.   O they tell me of a home
where my friends have gone,
O they tell me of that land far away,
Where the tree of life
in eternal bloom
Sheds its fragrance thro' the unclouded day.

    CHORUS

3.   O they tell of a King
in His beauty there,
And they tell me that mine eyes
shall behold
where He sits on the throne that is
whiter than snow,
In the city that is made of gold.

    CHORUS

4.   O they tell me that He
smiles on His children there,
And His smile drives their
sorrows all away;
And they tell me that no tears
ever come again,
In that lovely land of
unclouded day.

    CHORUS

Sweet Hour Of Prayer

Wm. B. Bradbury

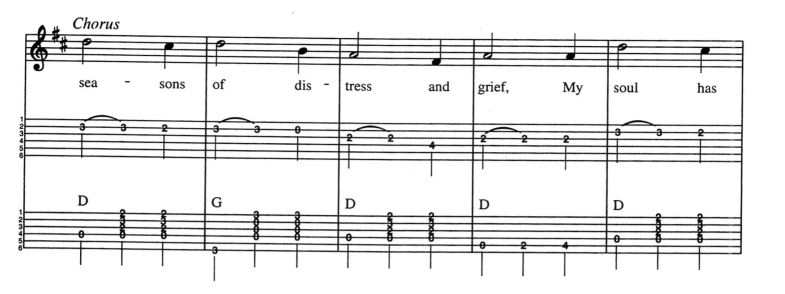

Sweet Hour Of Prayer

Arr. by Steve Kaufman

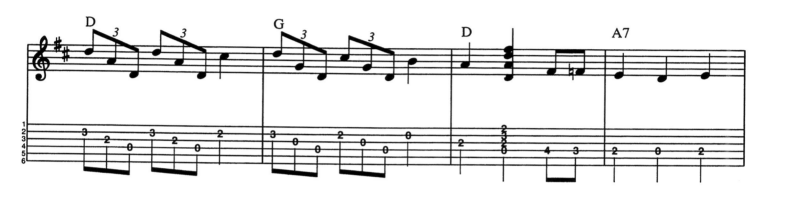

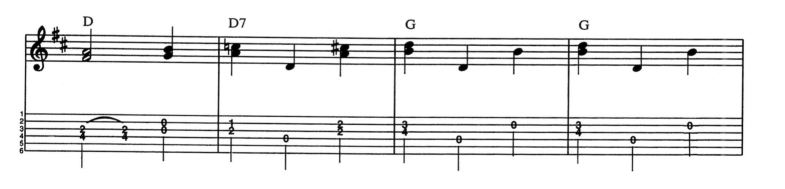

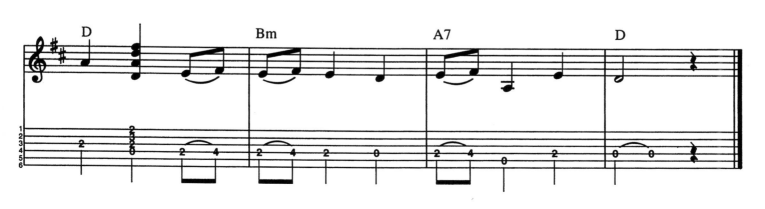

Sweet Hour Of Prayer

1. Sweet hour of prayer! Sweet hour of prayer!
   That calls me from a world of care,
   And bids me at my Father's throne
   Make all my wants and wishes known;
   In seasons of distress and grief,
   My soul has often found relief,
   And oft escaped the tempter's snare
   By thy return, sweet hour of prayer.

2. Sweet hour of prayer! Sweet hour of prayer!
   Thy wings shall my petition bear
   To Him whose truth and faithfulness
   Engage the waiting soul to bless;
   And since He bids me seek His face,
   Believe His Word and trust His Grace,
   I'll cast on Him my every care,
   And wait for thee, Sweet hour of prayer.

3. Sweet hour of prayer! Sweet hour of prayer!
   May I thy consolation share,
   Till, from Mount Pisgah's lofty height,
   I view my home, and take my flight:
   This robe of flesh I'll drop, and rise
   To seize the everlasting prize;
   And shout, while passing through the air,
   Farewell, farewell, sweet hour of prayer.

Precious Memories

J. B. F. Wright

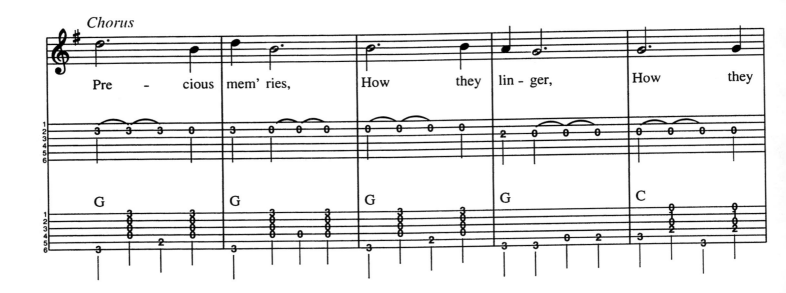

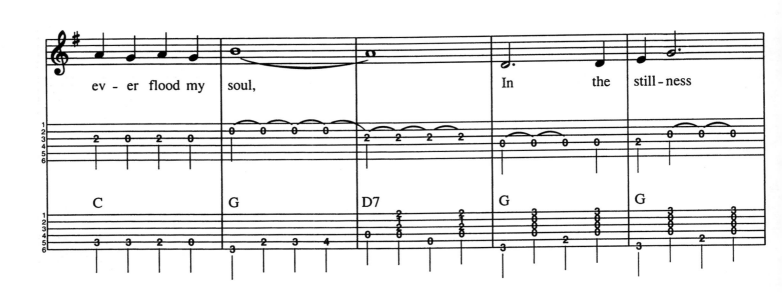

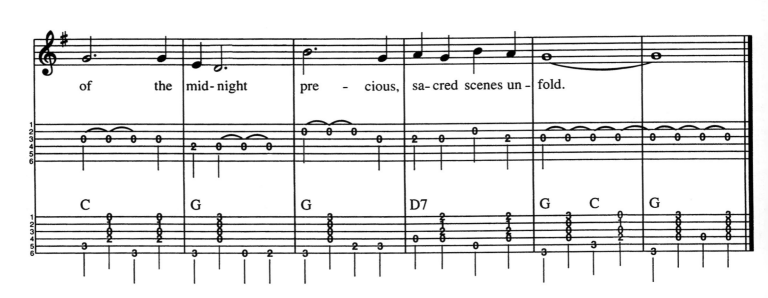

Precious Memories

Arr. by Steve Kaufman

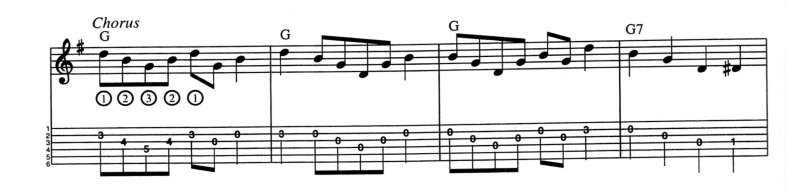

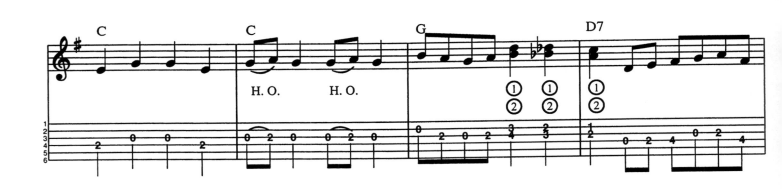

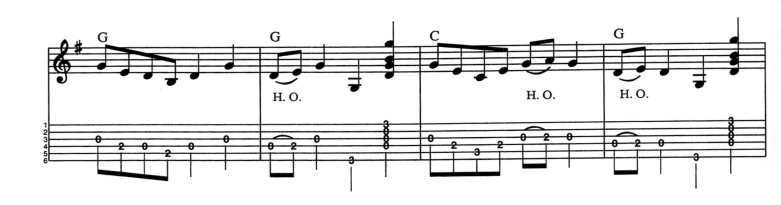

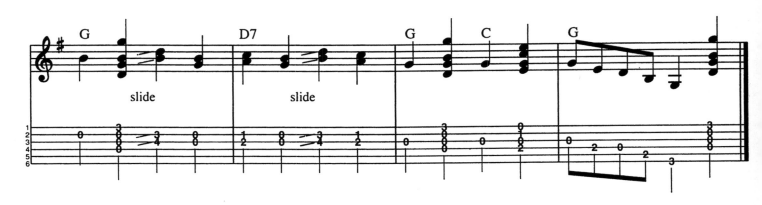

Precious Memories

1. Precious Mem'ries, unseen angels,
   Sent from somewhere to my soul;
   How they linger, ever near me,
   And the sacred past unfold.

REFRAIN
   Precious Mem'ries, how they linger,
   How they ever flood my soul;
   In the stillness of the midnight,
   Precious, sacred scenes unfold.

2. Precious Father, loving mother,
   Fly across the lonely years;
   And old home scenes of my childhood,
   In fond memory appear.

   CHORUS

3. In the stillness of the midnight,
   Echoes from the past I hear;
   Old time singing, gladness bringing,
   From that lovely land somewhere.

   CHORUS

4. As I travel on life's pathway,
   Know not what the years may hold;
   As I ponder, hope grows fonder,
   Precious memories flood my soul.

   CHORUS

Old Time Religion

Arr. by Steve Kaufman

Old Time Religion

Arr. by Steve Kaufman

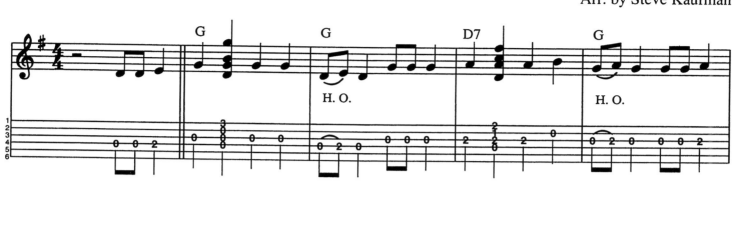

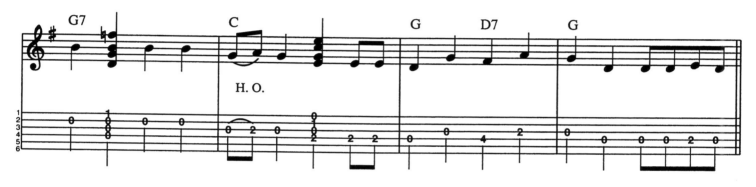

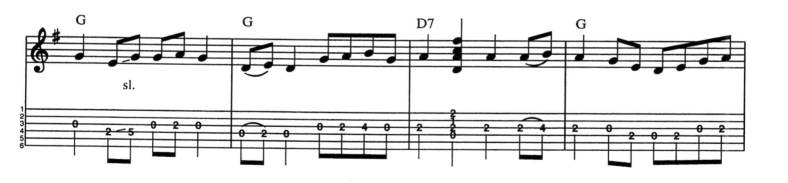

Old Time Religion

'Tis the old time religion,
'Tis the old time religion,
'Tis the old time religion,
It's good enough for me.

1. Makes me love everybody,
Makes me love everybody,
Makes me love everybody,
It's good enough for me.

2. It was good for our mothers,

3. It has saved all our fathers,

4. It will save all our children,

5. It was good for Paul and Silas,

6. It will do when I'm dying,

7. It will take us all to heaven,

The Old Rugged Cross

Rev. Geo. Bennard

Chorus

slain.　So I'll　cher-ish the　old　rug-ged　cross,　Till my

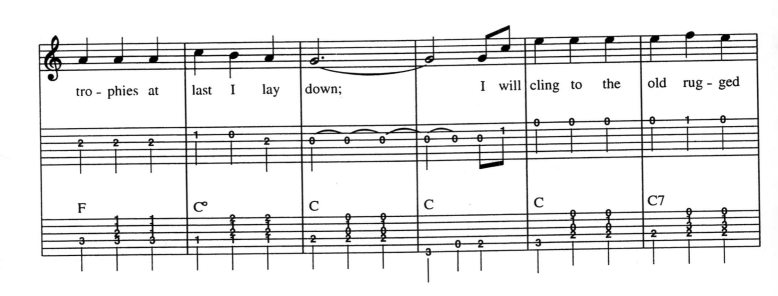

tro-phies at　last　I　lay　down;　I will cling to the　old　rug-ged

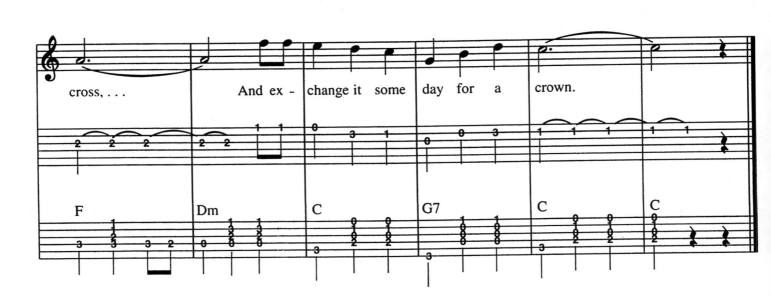

cross, . . .　And ex-change it　some　day　for　a　crown.

94

The Old Rugged Cross

Arr. by Steve Kaufman

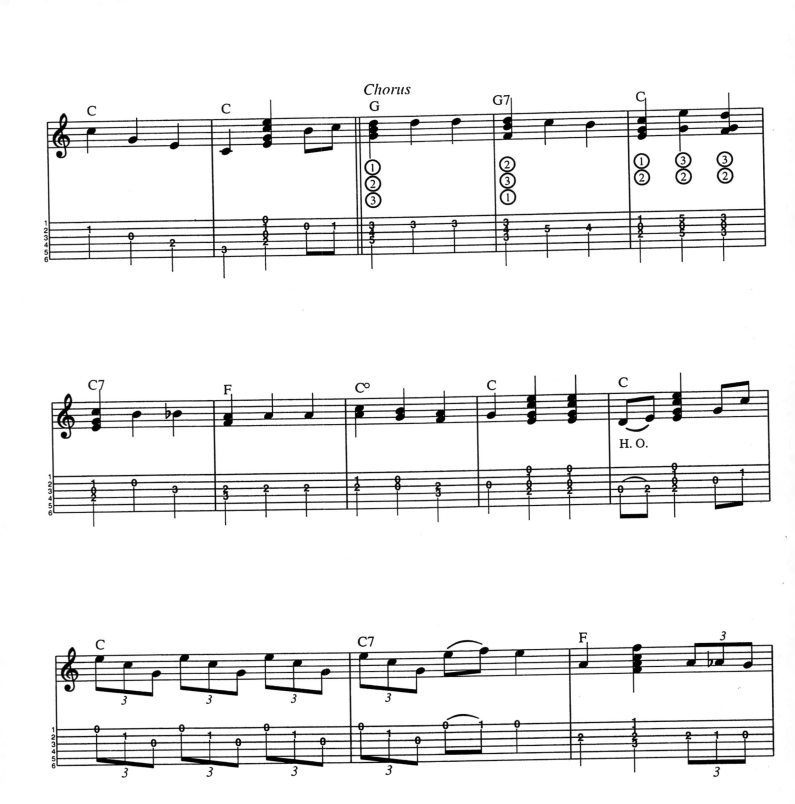

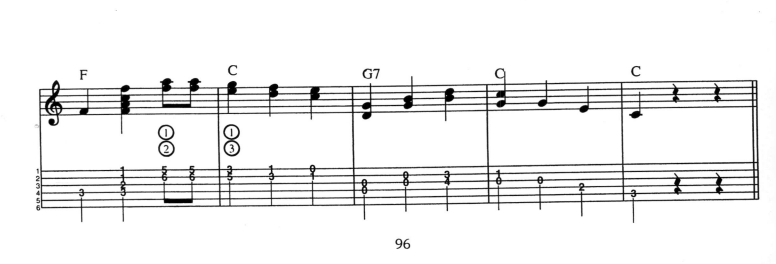

The Old Rugged Cross

1. On a hill far away
   stood an old rugged cross,
   the emblem of suffering and shame;
   And I love that old cross
   where the dearest and best
   for a world of lost sinners was slain.

CHORUS
   So I'll cherish the old rugged cross, . . .
   Till my trophies at last I lay down;
   I will cling to the old rugged cross, . . .
   And exchange it some day for a crown.

2. Oh, that old rugged cross,
   so despised by the world,
   has a wondrous attraction for me;
   For the dear Lamb of God
   left His glory above,
   to bear it to dark Calvary.

CHORUS

3. In the old rugged cross,
   stained with blood so divine,
   a wondrous beauty I see;
   For 'twas on that old cross
   Jesus suffered and died,
   to pardon and sanctify me.

CHORUS

4. To the old rugged cross
   I will ever be true,
   it's shame and reproach gladly bear;
   Then He'll call me someday
   to my home far away,
   where His glory forever I'll share.

The Old Gospel Ship

Arr. by Steve Kaufman

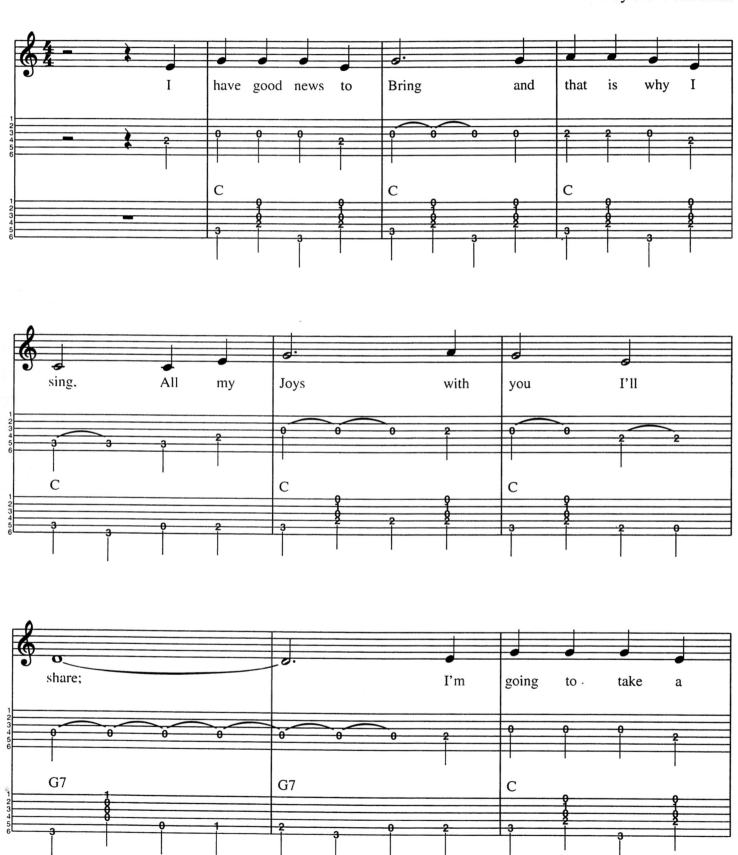

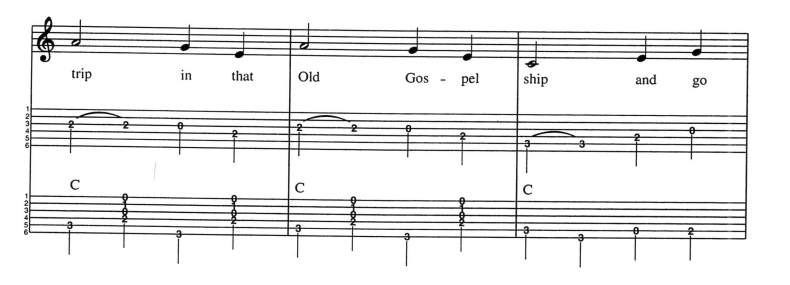

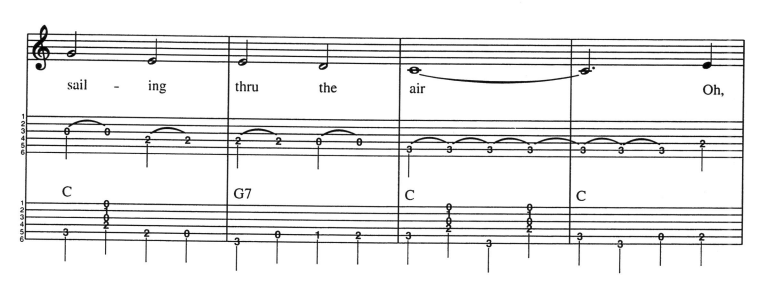

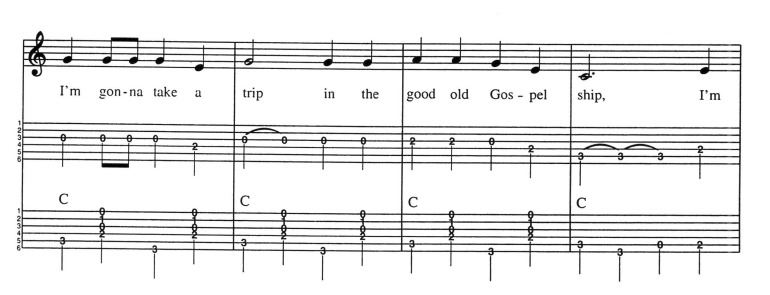

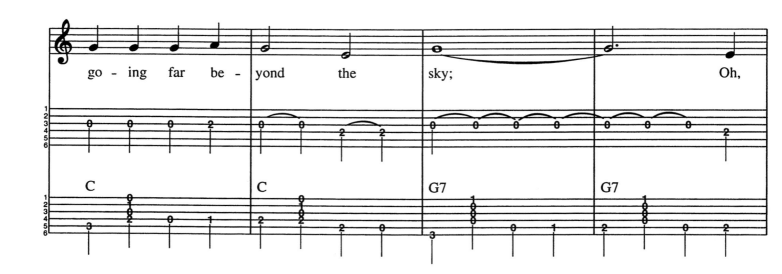

go - ing far be - yond the sky; Oh,

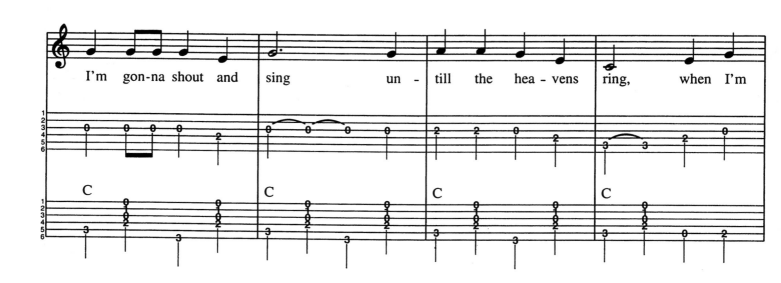

I'm gon-na shout and sing un - till the hea - vens ring, when I'm

Bidding this world Good Bye.

The Old Gospel Ship

Arr. by Steve Kaufman

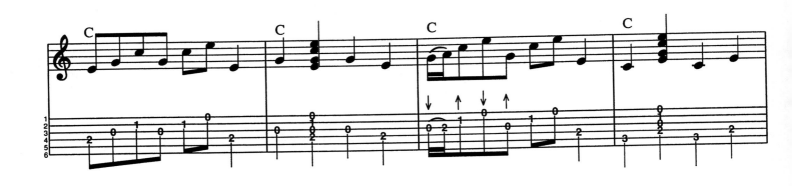

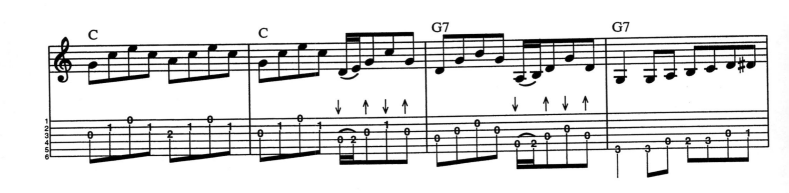

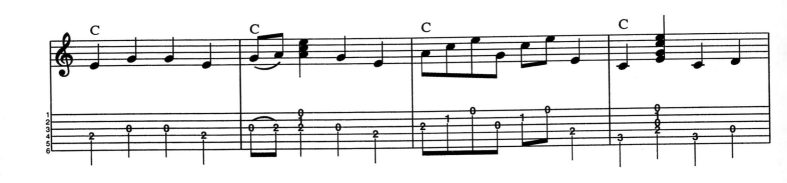

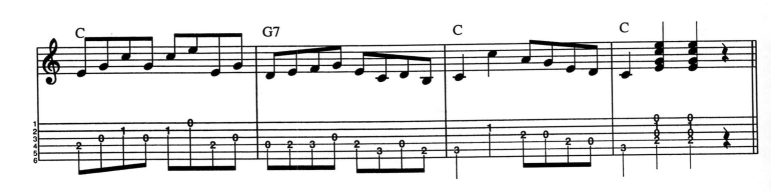

The Old Gospel Ship

1.   I have good news to bring,
and that is why I sing,
all my joys with you I'll share;
I'm going to take a trip,
in that Old Gospel ship,
and go sailing through the air.

CHORUS

    Oh, I'm "gonna" take a trip,
in that old gospel ship,
I'm going far beyond the sky;
Oh, I'm "gonna" shout and sing,
until the heavens ring,
when I'm bidding this world goodbye.

2.   Oh, I can scarcely wait,
I know I'll not be late,
for I'll spend my time in pray'r;
And when my ship comes in,
I will leave this world of sin,
and go sailing through the air.

    CHORUS

3.   If you're ashamed of me,
you have no cause to be,
for with Christ I am an heir;
If too much fault you find,
you will sure be left behind,
while I go sailing through the air.

    CHORUS

Sweet By and By

J. P. Webster

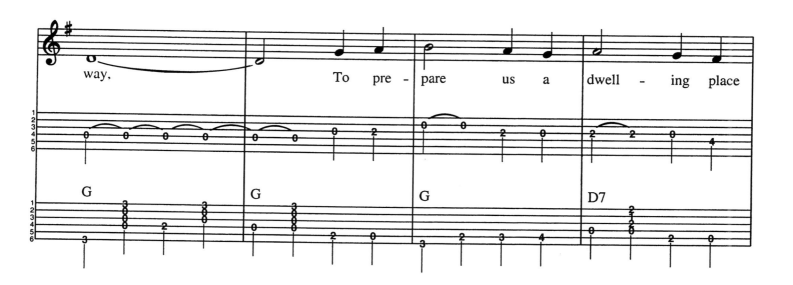

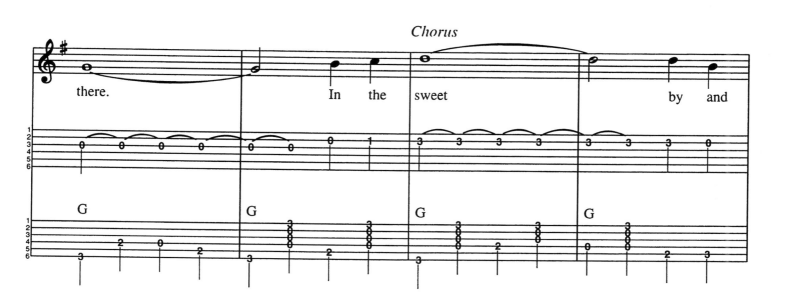

Chorus

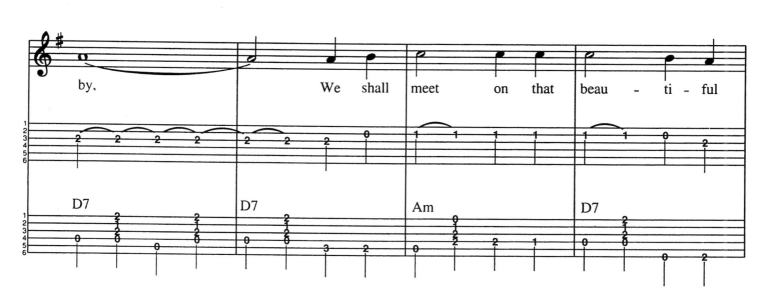

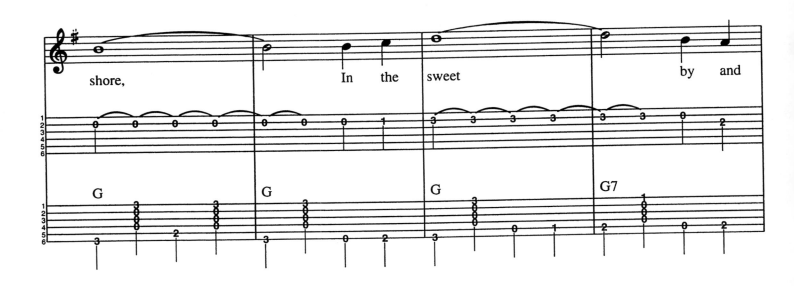

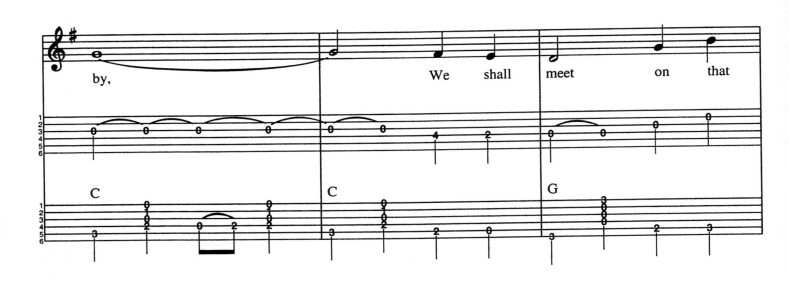

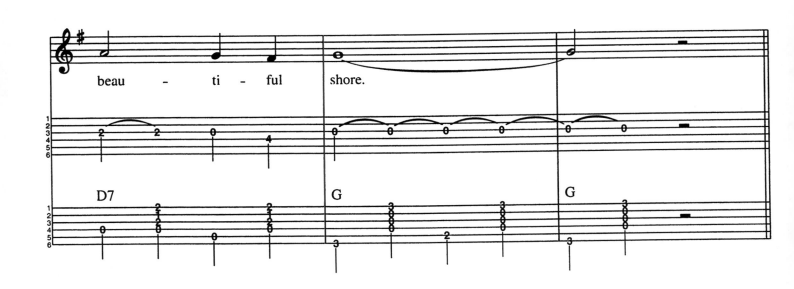

Sweet By and By

Arr. by Steve Kaufman

Sweet By and By

1.   There's a land that is fairer than day,
   and by faith we can see it afar;
   For the Father waits over the way,
   to prepare us a dwelling place there.

CHORUS
   In the sweet by and by,
   we shall meet on that beautiful shore;
   In the sweet by and by,
   we shall meet on that beautiful shore.

2.   We shall sing on that beautiful shore,
   the melodious songs of the blest;
   And our spirits shall sorrow no more,
   Not a sigh for the blessing of rest.

   CHORUS

3.   To the bountiful Father above,
   we will offer our tribute of praise;
   For the glorious gift of His love,
   and the blessings that hallow our days.

   CHORUS

Heaven's Jubilee

G. T. Speer

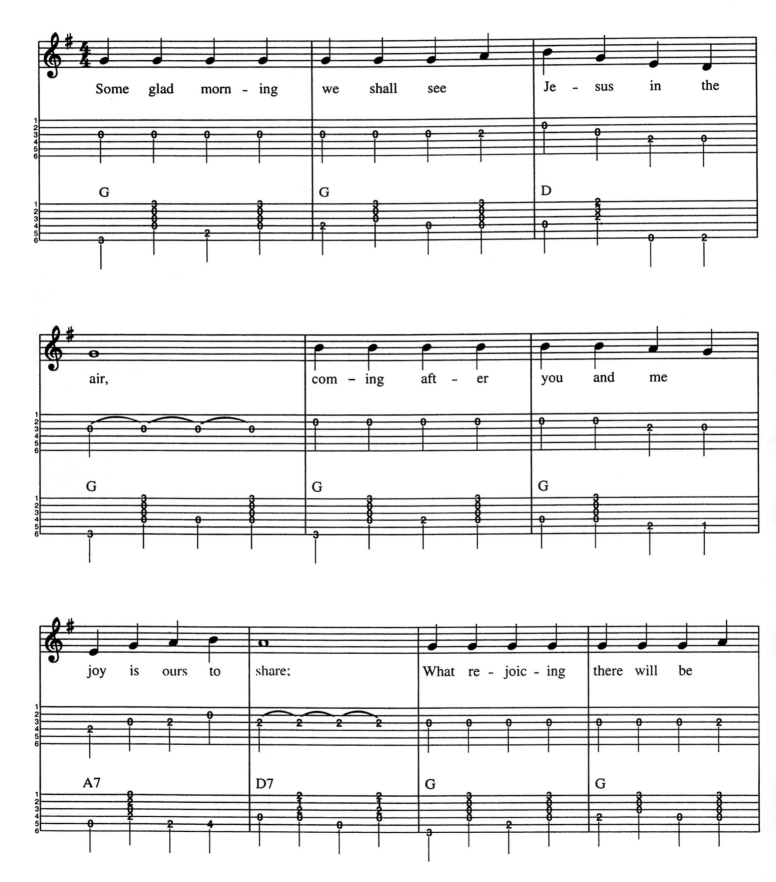

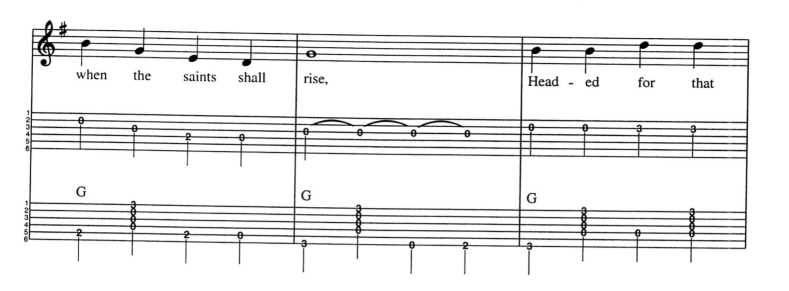

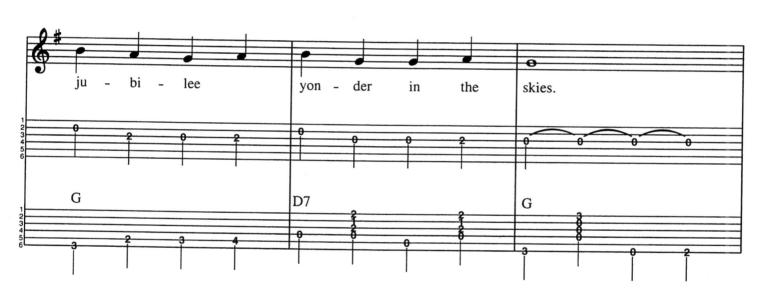

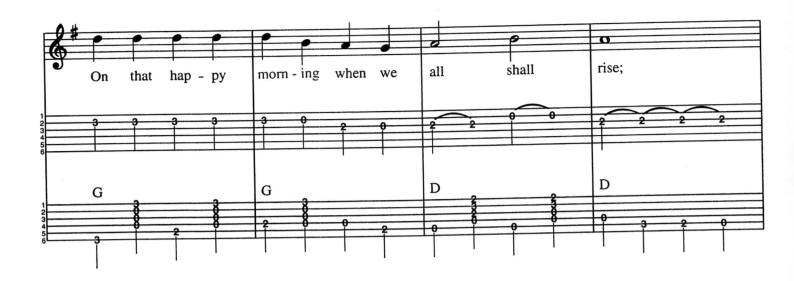

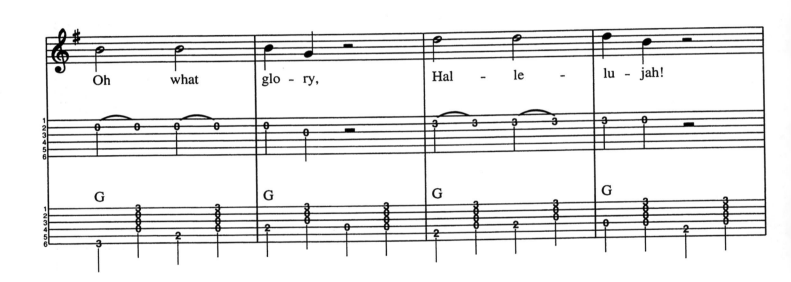

Heaven's Jubilee

Arr. by Steve Kaufman

113

Chorus

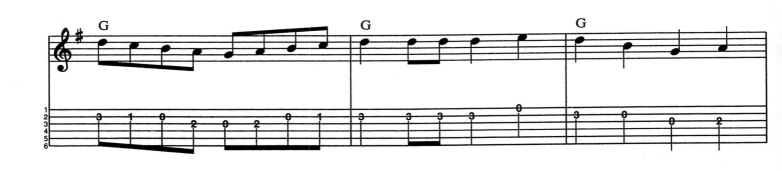

Heaven's Jubilee

1. Some glad morning we shall see
    Jesus in the air,
    Coming after you and me,
    joy is ours to share;
    What rejoicing there will be
    when the saints shall rise,
    Headed for that jubilee,
    yonder in the skies.

CHORUS

    Oh, what singing;
    oh, what shouting,
    on that happy morning
    when we all shall rise;
    Oh, what glory,
    Hallelujah!
    when we meet our
    blessed Savior in the skies.

2. Seems that now I almost see
    all the sainted dead,
    Rising for that Jubilee,
    that is just ahead;
    In the twinkling of an eye
    changing with them be,
    All the living saints to fly
    to that Jubilee.

    CHORUS

3. When with all that heav'nly host
    we begin to sing,
    Singing in the Holy Ghost,
    how the heav'ns will ring;
    Millions there will join the song,
    when them we shall be,
    Praising Christ thru ages long,
    heaven's Jubilee.

    CHORUS

Just A Closer Walk With Thee

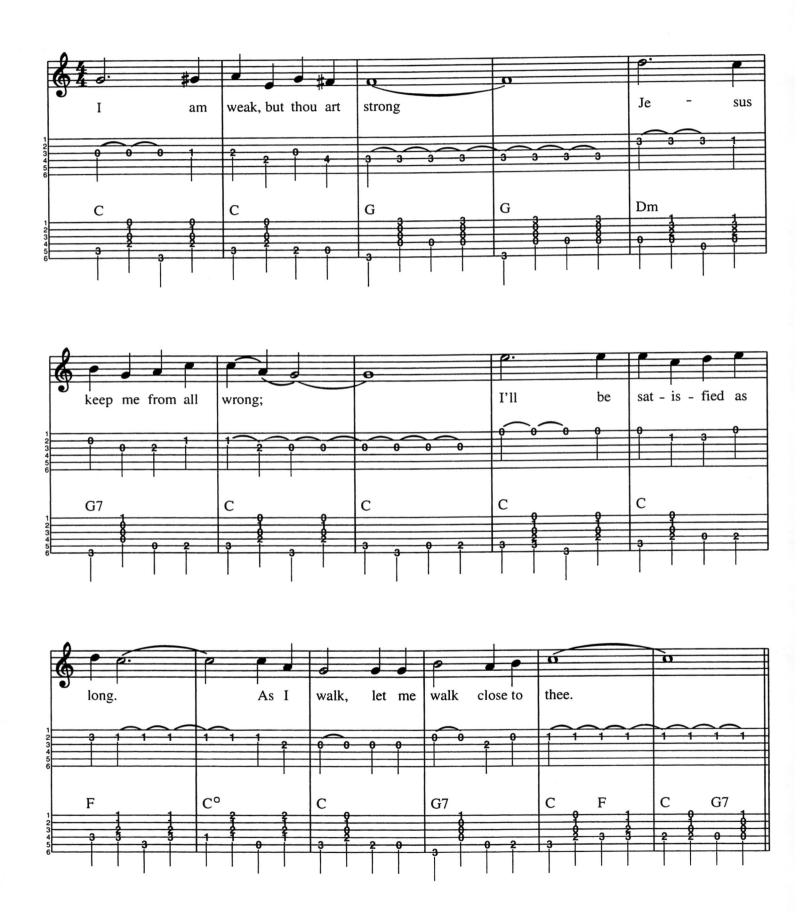

Chorus

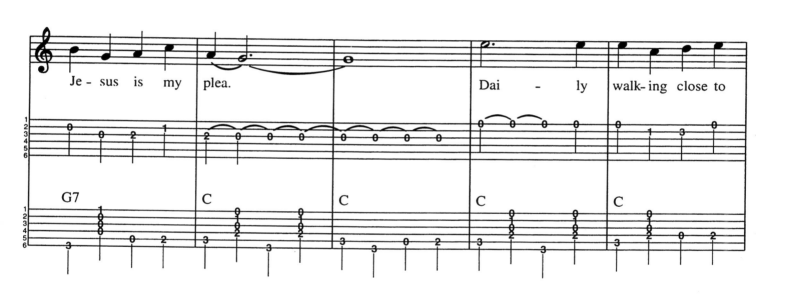

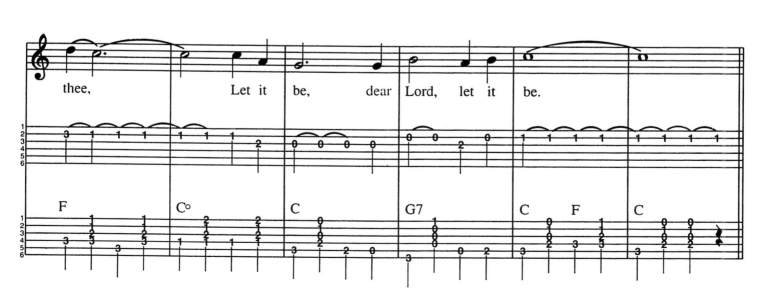

117

Just A Closer Walk With Thee

Arr. by Steve Kaufman

Just A Closer Walk With Three

1.   I am weak, but Thou art strong,
       Jesus keep me from all wrong;
       I'll be satisfied as long,
       as I walk, let me walk, close to Thee.

CHORUS
       Just a closer walk with Thee,
       Grant it Jesus, is my plea;
       Daily walking close to Thee,
       Let it be, dear Lord, let it be.

2.   Thru this world of toils and snares,
       if I falter Lord, who cares;
       Who with me my burden shares?
       None but Thee, dear Lord, none by Thee.

       CHORUS

3.   When my feeble life is o'er,
       time for me will be no more;
       Guide me gently, safely o'er,
       to my home on the bright golden shore.

       CHORUS

4.   When life's sun sets in the west,
       Lord, may I have done my best;
       May I find sweet peace and rest,
       in that home, happy home, of the blest.

       CHORUS

In The Garden

C. Austin Miles

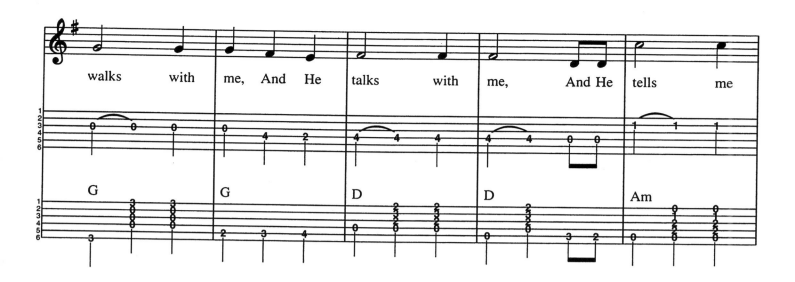

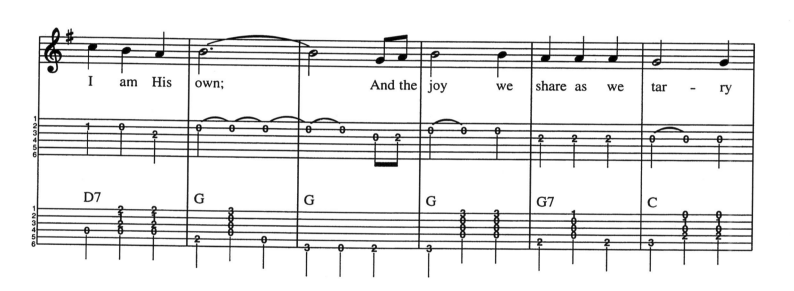

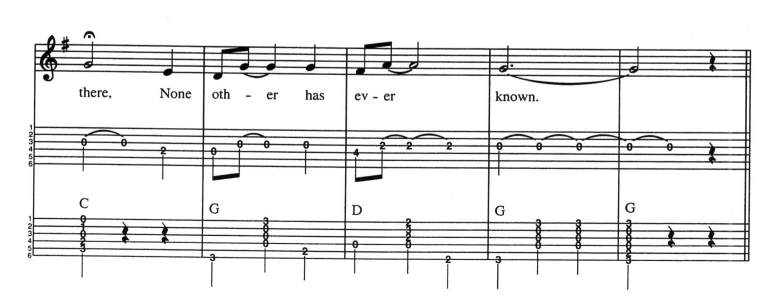

In The Garden

Arr. by Steve Kaufman

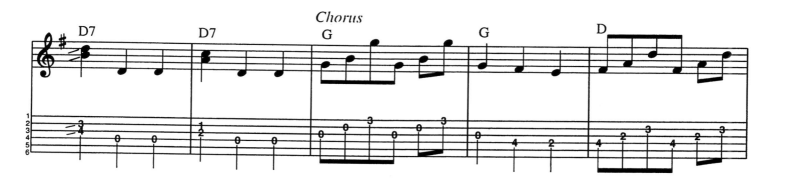

Chorus

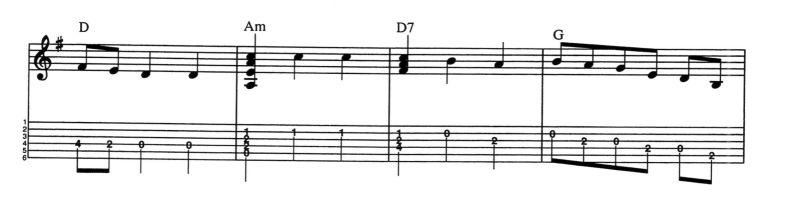

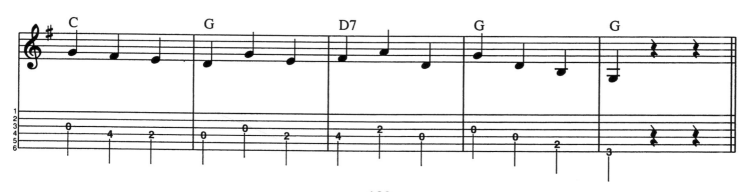

In The Garden

1. I come to the garden alone,
 while dew is still on the roses;
 And the voice I hear, falling on my ear,
 the Son of God discloses.

CHORUS
 And He walks with me,
 and He talks with me,
 and He tells me I am His own;
 And the joy we share,
 as we tarry there,
 none other has ever known.

2. He speaks, and the sound of His voice
 is sweet and the birds hush their singing;
 And the melody that He gave to me,
 within my heart is ringing.

CHORUS

3. I'd stay in the garden with Him,
 though the night around me be falling;
 But He bids me go, thru' the voice of woe,
 His voice to me is calling.

CHORUS

A Beautiful Life

Wm. M. Golden

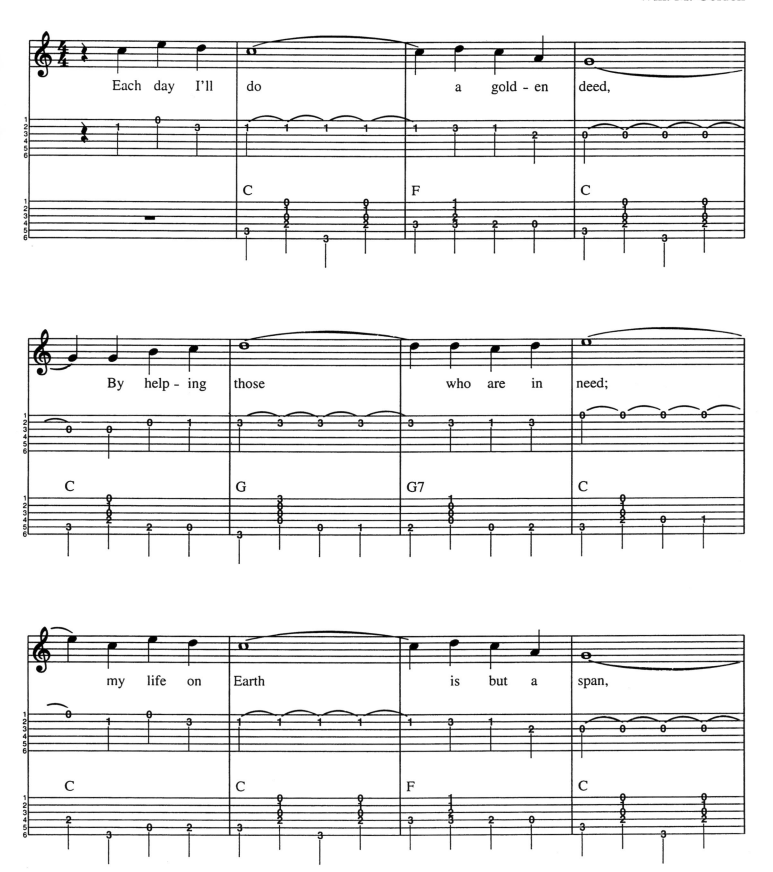

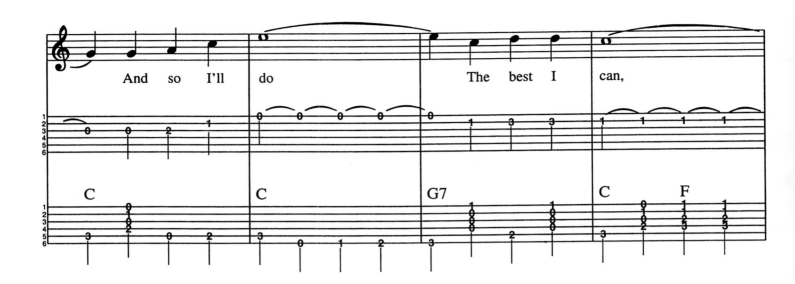

And so I'll do   The best I can,

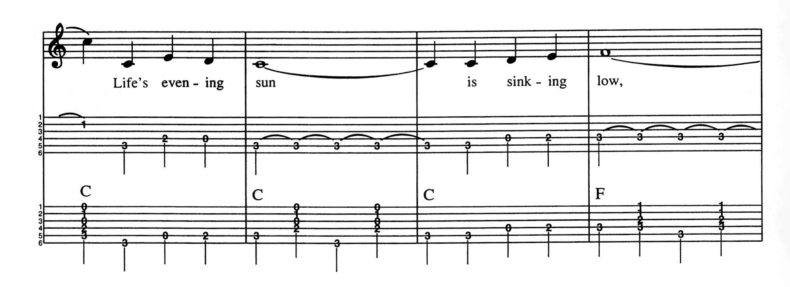

Life's even - ing sun   is sink - ing low,

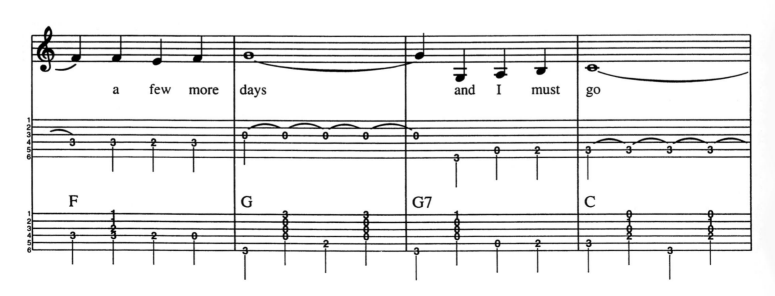

a few more days   and I must go

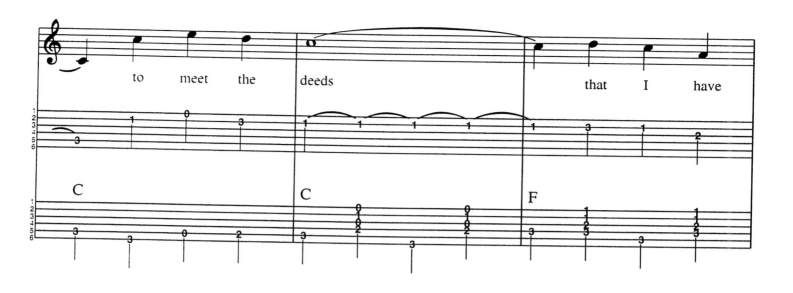

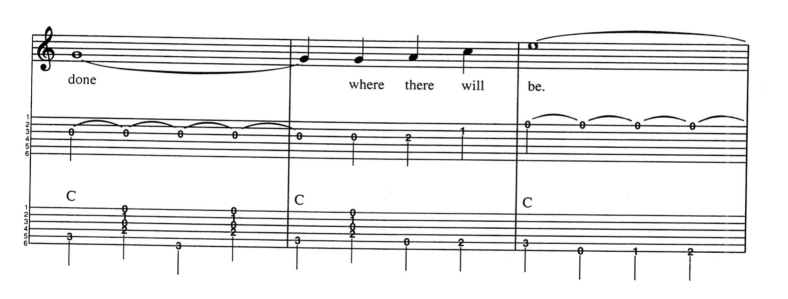

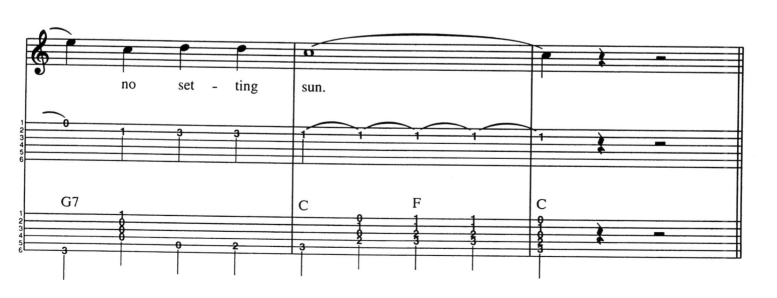

A Beautiful Life

Arr. by Steve Kaufman

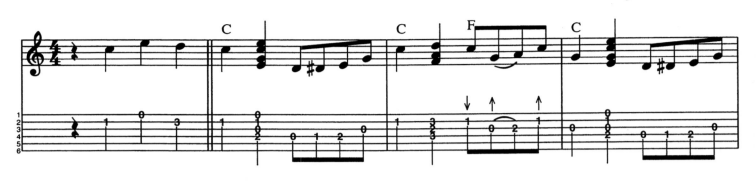

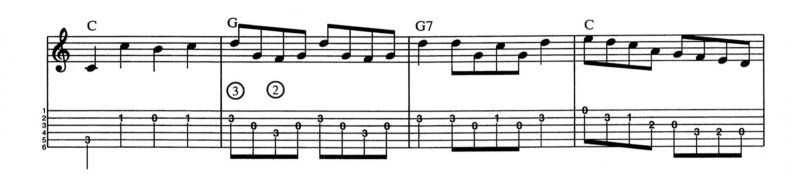

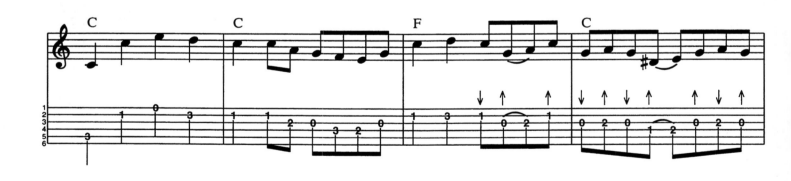

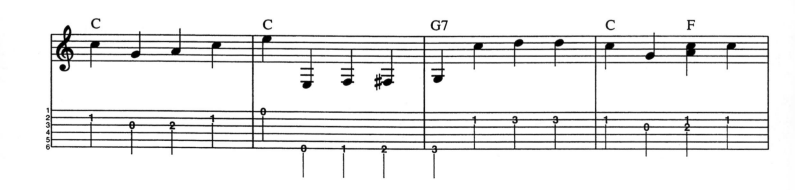

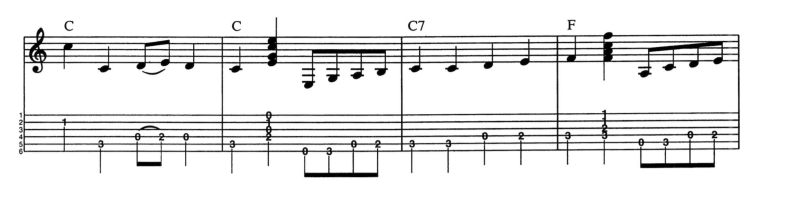

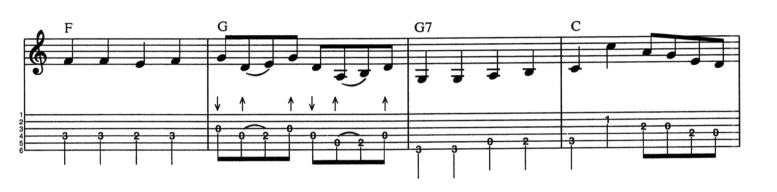

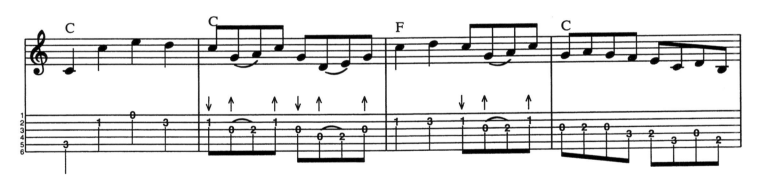

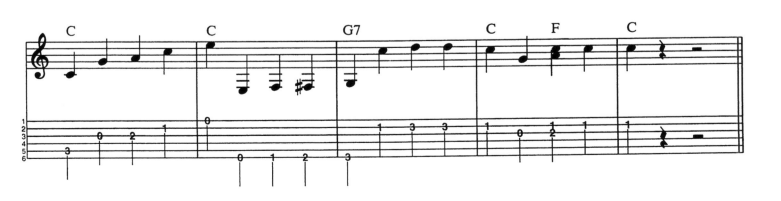

A Beautiful Life

1. Each day I'll do a golden deed,
    by helping those who are in need;
    My life on earth is but a span,
    and so I'll do the best I can.

CHORUS

>   Life's evening sun is sinking low,
>   a few more days and I must go;
>   To meet the deeds that I have done,
>   where there will be no setting sun.

2. To be a child of God each day,
    my light must shine along the way;
    I'll sing His praise while ages roll,
    and strive to help some troubled soul.

    CHORUS

3. The only life that will endure,
    is one that's kind and good and pure;
    And so for God I'll take my stand,
    each day I'll lend a helping hand.

    CHORUS

4. I'll help some one in time of need,
    and journey on with rapid speed;
    I'll help the sick, the poor and weak,
    and words of kindness to them speak.

    CHORUS

5. While going down life's weary road,
    I'll try to lift some trav'ler's load;
    I'll try to turn the night to day,
    and make flowers bloom along the way.

    CHORUS

There Is Power In The Blood

Lewis E. Jones

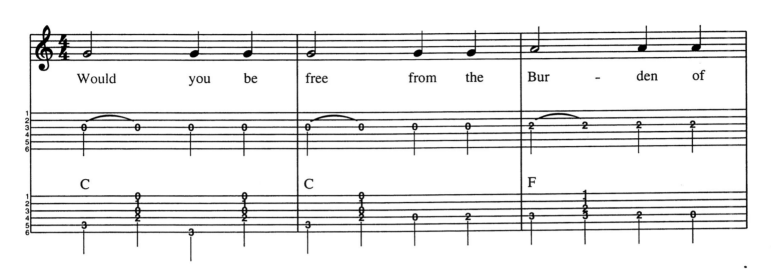

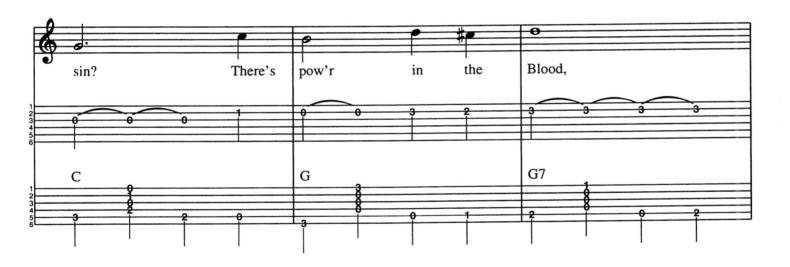

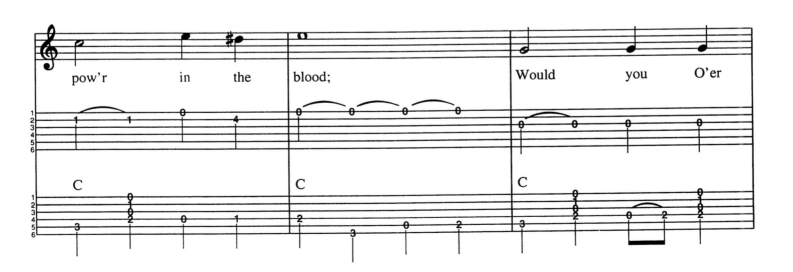

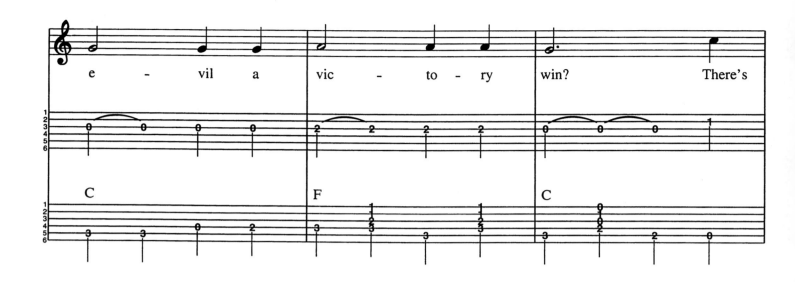

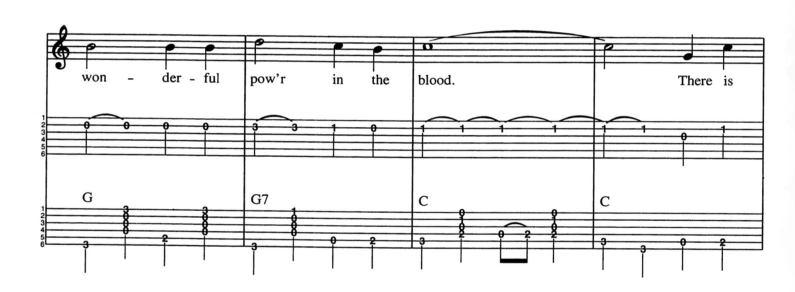

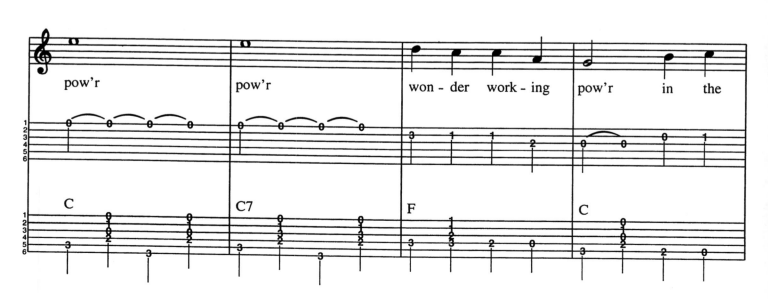

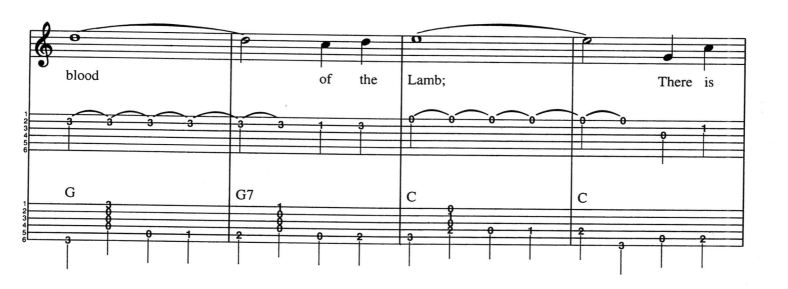

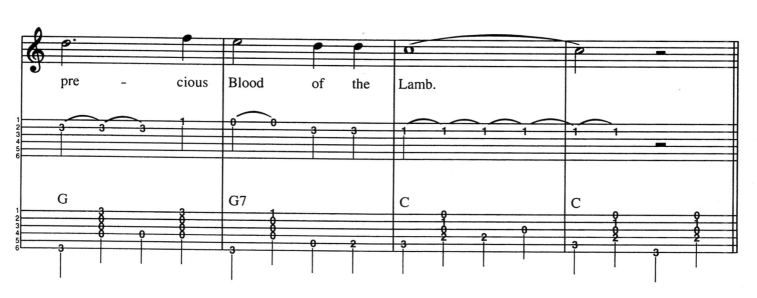

There Is Power In The Blood

Arr. by Steve Kaufman

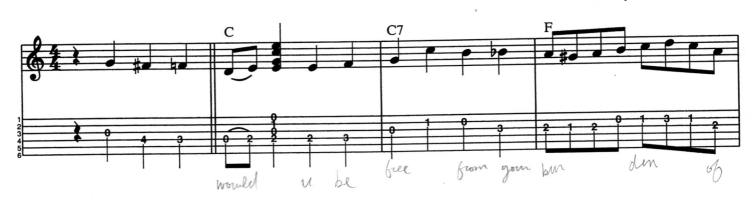

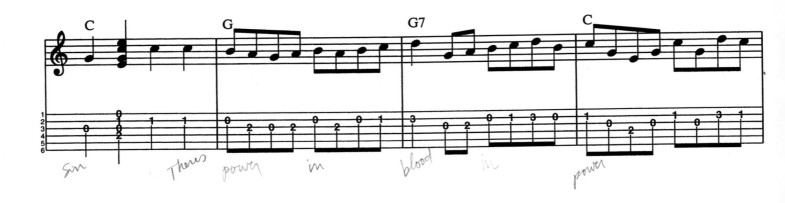

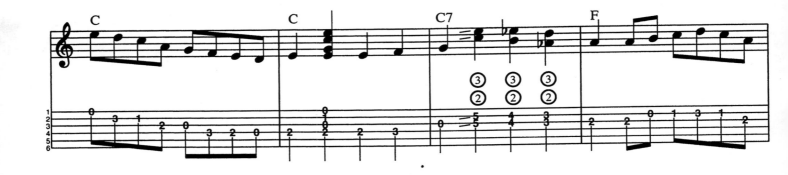

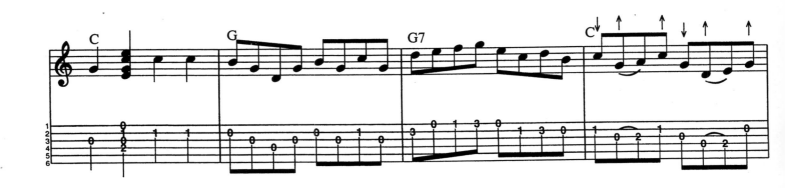

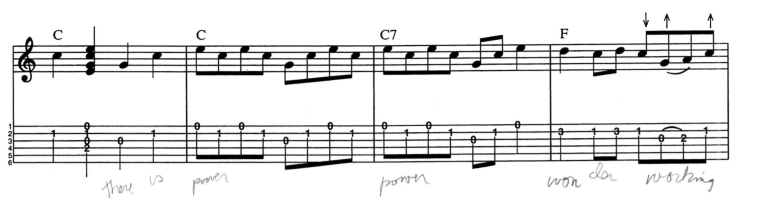

there is power power won der working

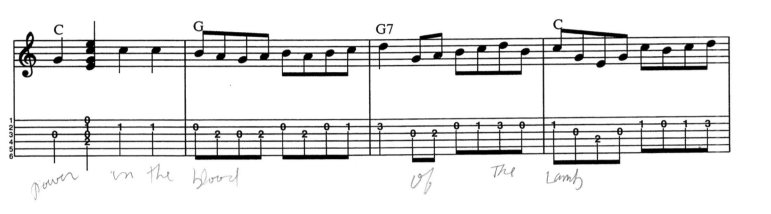

power in the blood of The Lamb

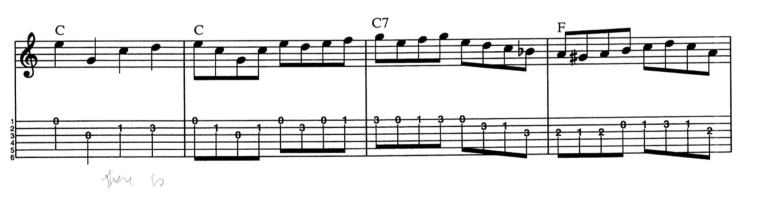

there is

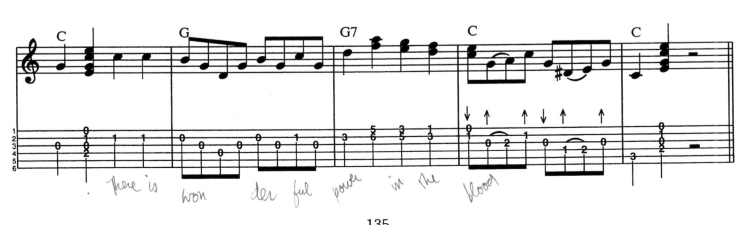

there is won der ful power in the blood

There Is Power In The Blood

1. Would you be free from the burden of sin?
   There's pow'r in the blood, pow'r in the blood;
   Would you o'er evil a victory win?
   There's wonderful pow'r in the blood.

CHORUS
   There is pow'r, pow'r, wonder working pow'r
   In the blood of the lamb;
   There is pow'r, pow'r, wonder working pow'r
   In the precious blood of the lamb.

2. Would you be free from your passion and pride?
   There's pow'r in the blood, pow'r in the blood;
   Come for cleansing to Calvary's tide?
   There's wonderful pow'r in the blood.

   CHORUS

3. Would you be whiter, much whiter than snow?
   There's pow'r in the blood, pow'r in the blood;
   Sin stains are lost in its life-giving flow,
   There's wonderful pow'r in the blood.

   CHORUS

4. Would you do service for Jesus your King?
   There's pow'r in the blood, pow'r in the blood;
   Would you live daily His praises to sing?
   There's wonderful pow'r in the blood.

   CHORUS

Pointers and Tips
For the Intermediate Solos

When The Roll Is Called Up Yonder

In the first measure you will find a "double stop," or two notes to be hit at the same time, slide. Use the first and second finger on the left hand to hold this slide. Many people try to use the third and fourth finger. I prefer the first and second because I can aim them more quickly. I practice this technique throughout most of this book when I am playing on two strings that are one fret apart.

Measure 15 will have two up swings in a row because of the eighth note hammer-on. Follow the arrows.

The chorus begins with the first finger holding down the first and second string and the second finger holding down the third string. This will form a partial F chord at the third fret.

Measure three of the chorus is like holding a D chord at the 7th fret. This is another way to hold a G chord. Measure 5 of the chorus is held with either two or three fingers. See which works best for you. Be sure to hold these positions, it will make it so much easier in these measures.

Watch out for the fingering in the last D7 measure.

The Glory-Land Way

Measure 5 has slide from the second to the fifth fret on the fourth string. Be sure to sustain this slide. In other words, hold the fifth fret as long as possible after the you slide. It will ring longer and sound fuller.

Measure 5 of the chorus has a slide from the second to the fourth fret on the third string. Use the second finger for this. When you get to the fourth fret, leave it down and use your first finger to fret the next note. Now flatten out your first finger and bar the first and second string. Hit the two strings as if they were one and hammer on your third finger onto the fifth fret on the second string. Make sure not to touch the first string when you perform the hammer-on so that the two notes will ring throughout the entire maneuver.

Life's Railway To Heaven

Hold down as many of the chord positions as you can. Notice the measures that have strums in them. In order to make this sound smooth and casual, you must hold the chord before you need it and leave it ringing after you hit it. Don't just hit the chord and release.

There are many crosspicking measures. They can be spotted by the repeating pattern of notes. Hold down all of the notes in the measure and roll the right hand in a down-up motion.

Measure 29 is a tricky one. Slide into the G position at the third fret. Watch out for the down-up motion.

Are You Washed In The Blood

Not much to report about this one. If you've practiced all of the techniques so far, you should have no trouble.

Nearer, My God, To Thee

Measure 7 has a tricky spot. Hit the D7 chord. Leave your first and second finger on the second and third strings, respectively, and try to get your third finger over to the fourth string about half a second after you strum. Hit the fourth string on an up-swing and hammer onto the fourth fret with your fourth finger. Then swing up onto the second fret on the third string. All of this takes place in about one and a half seconds. It's a piece of cake.

Faith Of Our Fathers

One of the hardest parts of this piece is holding, strumming and sustaining the chord while you hit the notes that follow the strum. These measures are: 1 through 4, 7 through 12, 15 through 19, and measure 22. Be sure to let the chord ring as long as possible.

Near The Cross

The same sustaining chord principle as "Faith Of Our Fathers" applies here. Seek out the measures that have sustaining chords in them and be ready for them. Sustaining the chords and notes will make you an all around smoother sounding guitarist.

Softly and Tenderly

There are many "double stop" measures in this piece. As we have discussed earlier, if the notes are just one fret apart then the fingers used are probably the first and second.

The chorus starts with a "double stop" that is two frets apart. I use the first and third fingers in this situation. You can use the second and fourth fingers also.

If two notes are found on top of each other, as in measures 5 and 6 of the chorus, then use the second finger on top of the third. Do not use one finger to fret both notes.

The Lily Of The Valley

This is the only tune in the book written in the key of A. The key of A has three sharps—F#, C# and G#. Most of the notes that you need to hit will be on the 2nd, 3rd, 4th and 5th frets. This means that you will be in second position with the first finger hitting the 2nd fret, second finger hitting the 3rd fret, third finger on the 4th fret and the fourth finger on the 5th fret. There are very few 1st frets. When they do occur, simply shift your hand back to first position until the next possible shift back to second position. Be sure to pay attention to the right hand's down up motion.

Where The Soul Never Dies

This tune is written out in the key of F in the Hymn Book so I kept it in the same form. Playing in the key of F is much like playing in the key of C. In measure 3 you have to hold down a two finger F chord. It is held like the two finger G chord that we used in some of the earlier pieces. Measure 5 and 11 use the same chord position. Strike the strings with the pick about a half of an inch away from the bridge in the cross picking measures. It makes the attack a little stiffer and tends to make the notes more distinct. Watch out for the places that have arrow marks. Following these pick strokes will make getting through these sections a little easier. Check out some of my other instructional material for some more tunes in the key of F.

When The Saints Go Marching In

There is not a whole lot to say about this piece except that it will prove itself challenging and fun to play. Watch out for measures 8 and 9. Measure 8 has a double stop slide in it. Play it in the same manner as we discussed earlier. The slide in measure 9 is played by holding down the E note on the 4th string–2nd fret. Hit the E note and the third string open at the same time and slide up to the 5th fret–4th string. Be sure not to touch the 3rd string while you slide. This would make the 3rd string stop ringing prematurely.

Measure 15 has a tricky right hand spot. Follow the arrows and you'll make it through this measure smoothly.

What A Friend

This is a tune that also appears in my Homespun Tapes instructional video—*Easy Gospel Guitar* (see the discography). It is a slow tune, so speed will not be an issue. Cleanliness might be, but speed should not. Watch out for the frequent hammer-ons. They should not be a fast movement. Many of my students try to rush the hammer-ons and pull-offs. The best way to get used to the speed of either of these is to hit the eighth note hammers or pulls with a down/up swing as if they were regular eighth notes and not hammer-ons. This will give you a better idea of the timing of these passages.

The second measure of the chorus is a different G7 formation. Hold down both of the 3rd fret notes so that all of the notes in the measure sound like open strings. This should happen in all cross picking measures.

Measures 3, 4 and 5 are crosspicking measures. Hold all of the notes in the whole measure that are used in the roll.

The Unclouded Day

The most difficult areas of the first 12 measures are the hammer-ons and double stops and slides. They have been covered in earlier pieces and don't really need to be covered here.

Measure 13 is made easy by means of the set-up. Use the fingerings that are marked. Start measure 13 with the third finger hitting the first note, then shift your third finger over to the 3rd fret—1st and 2nd string. Hold both notes with the flat of the 1st finger, like a bar. Hit both strings like any other double stop. The measure ends with a hammer-on by hitting the 1st and 2nd string—third fret, and hammering the third finger onto the fifth fret—second string. Be sure not to touch the 1st string with your third finger when performing the hammer-on. You want to be able to hear both strings through this maneuver.

Measure 1 and 5 of the chorus have this same hammer-on.

Sweet Hour Of Prayer

This melody is written out in the key of D. It is also a slower tune so don't race through or rush anything. The only difficult passages to point out are the measures that have triplets in them. In the case of triplets the three notes will get one full beat. They are very hard to time out so try to play along with the tape. Have fun with this one. I have.

Precious Memories

"Precious Memories" is one of my favorite gospel tunes to play. It can be played very gothically, jazzy and, depending upon where you are playing this tune, very bluesy.

Measure 5 has a hammer-on in the middle of a set of eighth notes. Follow the arrow markings. This same right hand technique of two up swings in a row can be found in measure 7. Use the fingerings that are marked.

Hold an F chord at the third fret to start the chorus. You will not have to bar the 1st string.

Watch out for the single and double stop slides in this piece.

The Old Rugged Cross

This tune is in 3/4 time. Play it slowly and make sure that all of your notes ring like open strings. This will give you more sustain and make the overall sound much smoother.

Measure 2 has a tricky maneuver in it. You have to strum through the C chord and then reach your little finger out to the 4th fret and come up on it. They are eighth notes so they will go pretty quickly.

Measure 3 has a triplet hammer-on in it. Play it smoothly and watch the arrows.

Watch out for the fingerings in measures 13 and 14.

Measure 1 and 2 of the chorus are difficult to make sound smooth. Hold the whole chord for each measure. Use the fingerings as they are marked.

Measures 9 and 10 of the chorus are filled with triplets. They should be steady and smooth. When you play triplets you should say to yourself "1 2 3 1 2 3 1 2 3".

The Old Gospel Ship

Here is a peppy tune for you. The verse is played just about like the chorus. The melody for both parts is the same. I don't foresee any trouble through the verse so we will skip onto the chorus.

Measure 1 of the chorus has a different crosspicking pattern than the others we have done. Take your time and work this measure out.

Measure 3 of the chorus is a crosspicking measure with a 16th note hammer-on sandwiched in the first beat. Count this measure out and listen to the tape and you'll get the hang of it. This same 16th note hammer-on is in several measures of this tune. Work on them until they smooth out.

Sweet By and By

All of the difficult sections up to measure 6 have been covered earlier. At the end of measure 6 is a two-up-swing, in-a-row hammer-on. This is followed by a two-up-swing, in-a-row pull-off. Follow the arrows and you won't have any trouble.

Measure 2 of the chorus has a slide from the 4th to the 2nd fret. It is hard to get this motion smooth, but with a little practice you will be proficient at it. No other trouble spots spotted.

Heaven's Jubilee

Speed is a big factor in picking "Heaven's Jubilee." There are many slides and hammer-ons which will make playing the notes seem faster than it really is. I play all of the 2nd fret to 4th or 5th fret slides with my second finger (left hand). Watch out for the arrows in some of these trickier measures.

We have already gone over how to play the slide in the first measure of the chorus. Measure 3 of the chorus can be performed two ways: either by using the first finger for both notes, starting the slide on the 2nd fret, or by using the third finger on the 1st string together with the second finger on the 2nd string. Read that back and see if it made any sense.

Be sure to only play the 1st ending once and then repeat the chorus. Skip over the first ending and play the second ending.

Just A Closer Walk With Thee

There are not very many places that will give you trouble in this piece. The first place to watch is in measure 5. Hold down all of the different numbers in the measure. This will make up a D minor chord. Be sure to hold the whole chord down while playing this measure. You will get more sustain and the overall sound will be smoother. The same technique holds true for parts of measures 9 and 12.

You will find a hammer-on triplet in measure 13. Use your 2nd, 3rd and 4th fingers for this hammer-on and keep in mind that all three notes should be done within one full beat.

Use the first and second endings.

In The Garden

"In The Garden" is one of my newfound favorite tunes to play. It reminds me of when I learned how to play "Blackberry Blossom" or "Ragtime Annie" . . . I could sit and play them for hours.

The trouble spots in this tune start with the third measure. You must quickly slide the second finger from the second fret to the fourth fret, then swing up on the next note. The note that you are sliding from is called a grace note and it is barely heard.

Measure 4 has the same type of technique. The two measures should mirror each other.

Measures 3, 4, 9, 10, 13 and 14 of the verse, and measures 1, 3, 9, 10 and 11 of the chorus are best played by holding down all of the notes that don't change. This will give you a chord group or chord form to crosspick. As always, holding a chord while crosspicking will give the overall sound more sustain and make the piece flow.

Measure 9 of the chorus has a grace note slide like in the beginning of the song.

A Beautiful Life

This is a fun tune to play. It is played with a lot of spirit and bounce. The first troublesome measure is number 2. The little finger holds the 2nd string. The third finger holds the 4th string and the second finger holds down the 3rd string while the first finger stays on the 2nd string in ready.

Measure 5 has some fingering markings to look out for.

Watch out for the two up swings in a row in measures 2, 10, 11, 21, 25 and 26. Play these sections smoothly and clearly.

There Is Power In The Blood

You've made it all the way to the end of my *Flatpicking The Gospels*. Congratulations! By this time you need no more pointers on any runs or techniques covered in this flatpicking handbook. All of the hard spots in this tune have been covered in some of the other songs. They may not be in the same key or for the same chord pattern, but the basic maneuver will still be the same.

If you have any real trouble while working your way through this book, or any of my other instructional materials, please feel free to write to me through Mel Bay Publications, Inc., or directly to me in care of my Maryville address. I hope you have had fun picking through this book and will be on the lookout for more flatpicking books coming your way.

Best always,
Steve Kaufman
429 West Broadway
Maryville, Tennessee 37801

DISCOGRAPHY

For Your Listening Pleasure

To The Lady —*One of the most recent Steve Kaufman recordings. 58 minutes of hot fiddle tunes, ballads, 3 original instrumentals, 6 classic tunes. Lots of fun and great listening. Available in* **CD or long-playing cassette**

Breaking Out — *solo Steve Kaufman pickin'. Whiskey Before Breakfast, Jerusalem Ridge, The I Miss You Waltz, Temptation Rag, Faded Love, Turkey In The Straw and more.* **Now on CD and cassette**

Star of the County Down — *A HOT duo recording with 1985 National Flatpicking Champ Robin Kessinger. The World is Waiting For The Sunrise, Cattle In The Cane, Calgary Polka and more.* **Cassette only**

Frost On The Window — *A remixed and remastered 44-minute cassette from 1985 with two new cuts. Six tunes were recorded as they were played in the National Flatpicking Championships. Greensleeves, New Camptown Races, Red Wing, Alabama Jubilee, Grey Eagle, Black and White Rag plus 9 other selections.* **Cassette only**

Strange Company — *the four-piece jazz/swing band of which Steve is a member. Laid-back to high-energy. It's A Sin To Tell A Lie, Blue Moon, Walkin' After Midnight and many more.* **Cassette only**

An Evening With Steve Kaufman — *a 34-minute live show video. Lots of fun and close-up hot pickin'. Sally Gooden, Tattooed Lady, That's What I Like About The South and more.* **U.S. VHS format only**

For Your Instructional Needs

The Championship Flatpicking Guitar Book with a 1-hour cassette — *61 pages of advanced finger-burners. Some of the 16 tunes are: Beaumont Rag, Dill Pickle Rag, Grey Eagle, Sally Gooden and Farewell Blues.*

The Complete Flatpicking Guitar Book with a 1-hour cassette — *This book is for the* **beginner** *and is designed to take you all the way through the* **intermediate** *level to the edge of the* **advanced** *plane. 101 pages of tips and time-saving information. There are sections on bass walks, making your own arrangements to instrumentals and vocals, chord voicings, backup rhythm and brings you to the styles of Doc Watson, Norman Blake, Dan Crary, Tony Rice and Steve Kaufman.*

Bluegrass Guitar Solos That Every Parking Lot Picker Should Know Vol. 1 —*6 audio cassettes and a 165-page book of standard bluegrass* **Guitar Jamming Tunes** *written in notes and tablature. Learn to play: Ragtime Annie, Big Sandy River, Bill Cheatham, Billy In The Lowground, Gold Rush, Double Eagle, Flop-Eared Mule, Fisher's Hornpipe, Forked Deer, Blackberry Blossom, Old Joe Clark, Turkey In The Straw, Soldier's Joy, St. Anne's Reel, Nothing To It, Arkansas Traveller, Red-Haired Boy, Sweet Georgia Brown, Salt Creek and Whiskey Before Breakfast.* **Level: beginner, intermediate and advanced**

Bluegrass Guitar Solos That Every Parking Lot Picker Should Know Vol. 2 — *A sister series with the same format as Vol. 1. 6 cassettes with* **20 more standard tunes for you to learn.** *You will learn to play: Alabama Jubilee, Black Mountain Rag, Blackberry Rag, Cherokee Shuffle, Cricket On The Hearth, Dixie Hoedown, Down Yonder, Eighth of January, John Hardy, June Apple, Katie Hill, Liberty, Mississippi Sawyer, Peacock Rag, Red Wing, Stoney Creek, Temperance Reel, Texas Gales, Wheel Hoss and, yes, The Wildwood Flower.* **Level: beginner, intermediate and advanced**

What To Play When The Singing Stops–Bluegrass Guitar Solos That Every Parking Lot Picker Should Know Vol. 3. — *This is the same format as Vol. 1 and 2 except this series is designed to teach you to play the solos for 20 of the most standard bluegrass vocals. 115-page book with 6 cassettes.* **Level: beginner, intermediate and advanced**

Learn To Flatpick–The Video — *A video produced for the beginner and intermediate level. Lots of tips and time-saving remedies to many of the mysteries of guitar picking. Some of the tunes covered in this 90-minute video are The Wildwood Flower, Old Joe Clark and Down Yonder.* **Level: beginner/intermediate**

Easy Gospel Guitar–The Video — *Through this 90-minute video, you will learn to* **play bluegrass/country guitar through your favorite gospel songs.** *Whether you are a beginning or intermediate player, you will* **develop a repertoire** *of tunes and* **add style** *to songs you may already know. Steve slowly plays the accompaniment and melody of each song, then enhances the arrangement with* **basic chords, bass walks, hammer-ons, pull-offs, runs and other techniques.** *You'll soon be playing wonderful arrangements to these well-known tunes: Amazing Grace, Just A Closer Walk With Thee, Old-Time Religion, The Old Rugged Cross, Will The Circle Be Unbroken, What A Friend We Have In Jesus and Cryin' Holy Unto The Lord.* **Level: beginner/beginner-intermediate**

To order any of these Steve Kaufman Products write to:
Steve Kaufman
429 West Broadway
Maryville, TN 37801
or call 1-800-FLATPIK